Abstracts of

Adams County Pennsylvania

WILLS

1800-1826

Kevin Greenholt

HERITAGE BOOKS
2007

HERITAGE BOOKS
AN IMPRINT OF HERITAGE BOOKS, INC.

Books, CDs, and more—Worldwide

For our listing of thousands of titles see our website
at
www.HeritageBooks.com

Published 2007 by
HERITAGE BOOKS, INC.
Publishing Division
65 East Main Street
Westminster, Maryland 21157-5026

Copyright © 1988 Kevin Greenholt

All rights reserved. No part of this book may be reproduced or transmitted in any form or by any means, electronic or mechanical, including photocopying, recording or by any information storage and retrieval system without written permission from the author, except for the inclusion of brief quotations in a review.

International Standard Book Number: 978-1-58549-060-8

TABLE OF CONTENTS

Will Book A (1800-1807)...1 - 15
Will Book B (1807-1817)...16 - 37
Will Book C (1817-1826)...38 - 57
Surname Index...58 - 71
Additional Index Entries..72

WILL BOOK A

ADAIR, John - Liberty Twp. Wife: Sarah; children: James, Mary CAMPBELL, Hugh (now in Ireland), Blaney, Nancy, Jenet MULLAN, Hannah, William, Josiah, Sally; executors: Joseph MAGINNLY, James ADAIR of Franklin Co., Pa.; witnesses: William and James REED, Robert HOWIE; written: no date; probate: 29 Dec 1806; both executors renounced; William MCMULLAN and Samuel ADAIR appointed admins; recorded: pg 387

ARNDT, Jacob - Franklin Twp. Wife: Catharina; children: Peter, John, Catharina wife of Christian STOUT, Molley wife of Valentine OYLER, Barbara wife of Jacob OYLER, Juliann wife of John BUMBAUGH, Susanna wife of John RUOMMEL; executors: John ARNDT, son, and Jacob OYLER, son-in-law; witnesses: Henry HOKE, Adam SWOPE, Alexander RUSSELL; written: 27 Oct 1801; probate: 24 Nov 1802; recorded: pg 160

BAKER, John - Berwick Twp., farmer, sick. Wife: Barbara; children: Magdalene wife of John MILLER, Elizabeth wife of Ludwick WOLLET, George, Barbara wife of John JACOBS, Christina wife of John GOSSLER; grandchildren: Elizabeth and Jacob MILLER of Magdalene; executors: George BAKER, son and Jacob MILLER, son-in-law; witnesses: John MUMMERT, Tobias KEPNER; written: 21 Aug 1804; probate: 3 Oct 1804; recorded: pg 254

BEALS, Caleb - Huntington Twp. Son: Caleb; grandchildren: Mary, Thomas, James and David Stockton BEALS of Caleb; executor: son Caleb; witnesses: William WIERMAN, Lydia ALTEMAS, Nathan SELLERS; written: 6 Aug 1804; probate: 17 Jun 1805; recorded: pg 298

BECHER, Henry - Petersburg, Germany Twp., frail. Wife: Catharine; children: Peter and others (unnamed); grandson: John WINTEROTH; executors: John and William BECHER, sons; witnesses: Robert MCILHINNY, Adam WINTRODE Jr; -- BRINGMAN; written: 23 Feb 1795; probate: 28 Jan 1807; recorded: pg 376

BERCAW, Margaret - Straban Twp., widow of George BERCAW. Children: Four daughters, named Magdalen, Ann HOUGHTALEN(?), sons; executors: Peter and George BERCAW, sons; witnesses: George WILLIAMSON, George BERCAW; written: 20 May 1801; probate: 6 Sep 1803; recorded: pg 211

BIGHAM, John - Liberty Twp. Siblings: Hugh, Robert, Thomas, William, McGurgon(?) BIGHAM, Margaret CALDWELL; nephews: David BIGHAM, blacksmith, John BIGHAM son of Thomas; niece: Agnes CALDWELL; executors: Mathias WINEBRIGHT, William BIGHAM; witnesses: David MARTIN, James MCKINLEY; written: 28 Nov 1803; probate: 7 Feb 1804; recorded: pg 224

BINDER, Magdalena - town of Berlin. Children: Peter, Ann wife of Gabriel SMITH Esq., Elizabeth wife of Emanuel SMITH; daughter-in-law: Margaret alias Rebeckah BINDER; granddaughters: Magdalena BINDER, Magdalena SMITH; executor: Valentine PRESSEL, Washington Twp., York Co.; witnesses: Frederick ASPER, William PATTERSON; written: 16 Dec 1804; probate: 26 Nov 1805; recorded: pg 325

BOWER, Michael Sr. - Warrington Twp., Adams County (York). Children: Benjamin, Jonathan, Catherine wife of Henry TROUP, Sarah, Elizabeth, Mary wife of Lenhart SHIMP, Rebecca wife of Michael MEYER; grandson: Michael of Jonathan; executor: son Benjamin; witnesses: Michael FORNER, Herman BLAESSER, Andrew BOWER, written: 6 Nov 1806; probate 26 Sep 1807; recorded: pg 427

BRICE, James - Hamiltonban Twp. Wife: Jane, to receive servant girl Mary RYON; children: Alexander, James; executors: wife Jane, son Alexander, David BLYTHE; witnesses: Robert SLEMMONS, J. MCGINLY, David HART; written: 21 Jan 1800; probate: 18 May 1800; recorded: pg 25

BROWN, Alexander - Tyrone Twp. Wife: Mary, to receive negro Phillis; children: Esther, Margaret wife of Samuel HADDEN, David (deceased), Samuel, Mary wife of Rev. Patrick DEVISON, James, John; children identified as by present wife: Samuel, Mary, James, David (another), John, Esther; son Samuel

1

WILL BOOK A

to receive negro Will; daughter Mary to receive negro Kate; executors: Samuel BROWN, son, and William GILLILAND; witnesses: Jacob MAY, Samuel and John GILLILAND; written: 3 Jun 1799; probate: 19 Apr 1800; recorded: pg 12

BROWN, Susanna - Germany Twp., widow. In German, not translated. Executor: Adam WINTERODE Jr.; witnesses: Adam WINTERODE Jr., Michael DEISERT; WINTERODE renounced, Henry KOHLSTOCK appointed admin; probate: 31 Jul 1805; recorded: pg 301

BUSHY, Peter - Reading Twp. Witnesses John PICKING and Jacob BUSHY certified that on Sunday 28 Oct 1804 they heard Peter BUSHY recite his will and that he died Sunday 4 Nov 1804. Will certified: 24 Nov 1804; recorded: pg 266

CAMPBELL, Hugh - Straban Twp., cabinet maker, very sick. Siblings: Margerett, Robert (deceased), Armstrong, Alexander and Mary CAMPBELL; children of Robert: Margerett, Robert and Anny; executor: Alexander CAMPBELL, brother; witnesses: William BOGLE, John WHITFORD; written: 8 Sep 1804; probate: 24 Feb 1807; recorded: pg 393

CASHMAN, Christian - Straban Twp., weak. Wife: Catharine; children: William, George, Barbara (deceased) wife of George HORN, Christian, Susannah wife of Philip HULL, John; grandchildren: Elizabeth CASHMAN, Catharine, George, Elizabeth and John HORN; indentured servants: Charlota HUET, Cathrana EABLE; executor: William CASHMAN, son; witnesses: Peter BEITLER, Henry SLAGLE; written: 6 Apr 1801; probate: 12 May 1801; recorded: pg 73

CLOPPER, Christina - no location, widow of Cornelius CLOPPER; son: Francis CLOPPER; step-son: Peter CLOPPER; brother: David CASSAT; nephews: Francis, Jacob, Peter, David and Henry CASSAT of deceased brother Peter; nieces: Christina CASSAT, daughter of Jacob, Christina MONFORT, daughter of sister Elisabeth and Lawrence MONFORT; bequest to Elizabeth wife of James MITCHELL; executors: Jacob CASSAT, brother, and David CASSAT son of brother David, they also named guardians of her son, Francis; witnesses: James ALLEN, Samuel PETERSON, Polly VANARSDAL; codicil mentions: John CLOPPER, no relationship stated, Sussan LOW widow of John LOW of New York, and Maria, wife of brother Jacob; written: 2 Jul 1799; probate: 24 Nov 1801; recorded: pg 101

COX, Naomi - Warrington Twp., Adams Co. (York), widow of William COX; daughters: Susanah widow of John GRIST; Ann wife of Thomas GRIST, Ruth wife of John WIREMAN, Ami wife of Jesse MARTIN; executors: Thomas PEARSON and Joshua COX, son; witnesses: Thomas VEELY, George GROUP, James NEETY; son renounced 18 Apr 1807; both renounced: 2 Jun 1807; John WIERMAN, John FICKES appointed admins 11 Jun 1807; written: 16 Oct 1806; probate: 27 Mar 1807; recorded: pg 395

DEGROFT, Margaret - Mt Pleasant Twp., sick. Children: Moses, Richard, Rachel, Mariah, Samuel, Nelly, Ane, Peggy, James; executors: son James, Henry BRINKERHOF; witnesses: Anne HOGHTALLEN, Mary JOHNSTON; written: 13 Jun 1807; probate: 18 Aug 1807; recorded: pg 419

DELAP, William - Tyrone Twp., weak. Wife: Ruth; children: John, Sarah widow of Stephen FALK, Robert, Mary wife of John WILLIAMSON, Samuel, George (deceased); grandchildren: William of George, Matthew JONES daughter of George; executors: son John, William GILLILAND; witnesses: Rudolph SPANGLER, Edward HATTON; written: 2 Jun 1805; probate: 1 Aug 1805; recorded: pg 306

DODDS, John - Tyrone Twp., yeoman, weak. Wife: Mary; children: Isabella MAXFIELD, Finly (deceased), Jane wife of William BRANDON, Agness, Mary, John, Sarah, Elizabeth; executors: daughter Agness DODDS, William MCGREW; witnesses: Nathan, Finley and Alexander MCGREW; written: 21 Apr 1800; probate: 26 Oct 1801; recorded: pg 93

WILL BOOK A

DORTITCH, Thomas - foot traveller, now in York (Adams) County, old and weak. Bequest to Jacob BELLENCE (PELLENTZ), Catholic priest, to say Mass each Friday for one year, but to have a High Mass at his burial; bequest to whomever was caring for him at his death and for taking his body to the Catholic Church for burial; bequest of a glass of --- 'to each that goith to my burial'; witnesses: Henry and David DANNER; written: 2 Feb 1795; probate: 12 Dec 1802; Jacob BOWER appointed administrator; recorded: pg 173

DOUGLASS, Thomas - Cumberland Twp. Wife: Susanna, to receive Negro wench Hannah; bequests to: niece Nelly DOUGLASS, youngest daughter of James; nephew James DOUGLASS, hatter, son of deceased brother Archibald; children of deceased sister, Elizabeth, formerly wife of John FURGUS; sister Ann wife of William WILSON; nephew Thomas of Robert DOUGLASS; executors: William MCGAUGHY, Alexander RUSSELL; witnesses: Archibald DICKEY, James SCOTT, James COBEAN; written: 2 May 1801; probate: 14 Aug 1802; recorded: pg 206

DUNWODDY, David - Cumberland Twp., blacksmith. Children: Mary wife of John WILLSON, David, Hugh, William, Nancy, Betsey, the last two to receive Negro Molly and their mother's share of John KERR's estate currently in hands of his nephews, James SCOTT and Hugh DUNWODDY; grandchildren: Sarah, Thomas, Jean, Nancy, Betsey WILLSON, David and Jean DUNWODDY of David, David CROSS son of Samuel CROSS, Jean, James and David of William and his wife Hannah; executors: son Hugh, Walter SMITH Esq.; witnesses: John and James GALLOWAY, Alexander RUSSELL; written: 16 Oct 1802; probate: 18 Dec 1802; recorded: pg 169

EHRMAN, Appolonia - Heidelberg Twp., weak. Father: Joseph EHRMAN, deceased; children of deceased sister Mary KLUNK wife of Joseph: Joseph, Peter, John, Mary, Teresa, Catharine; bequest to Rev. W. Francis X. BROSIUS; executor: brother Jacob KUHN; witnesses: Samuel and Henry LILLY; written: Mar 1800; probate: 5 Mar 1801; recorded: pg 63

ELDEN, William - Menallen Twp., yeoman, very sick. Wife: Martha; children: John, Robert, Joseph, Mary; brother-in-law Charles DELAP; executors: DELAP, Benjamin WRIGHT; witnesses: Jacob KOCH, Samuel HARLAN, Thomas COCHRAN; written: 3 Dec 1806; probate: 3 Feb 1807; recorded: pg 373

ERHART, Margaret - Reading Twp., widow. Children: mentioned with Elizabeth and Susannah named; executors: Henry NELL, Herman BLAESSER; witnesses: Jacob and Peter BUSHEY; written: 2 Jun 1804; probate: 24 Nov 1804; recorded: pg 265

ERWIN, Andrew - Straban Twp., sick. Wife: Sarah; children: Robert, Susannah DOUGHERTY, Jean wife of Henry OMMERMAN; grandsons: Andrew ERWIN/IRWIN and Andrew Erwin DOUGHERTY; apprentice: Thomas GREER; executors: son Robert, Alexander MCGREW; witnesses: William MCGREW, John BRINKERHOFF; written: 8 Oct 1802; probate: 11 Nov 1802; recorded: pg 153

EVERITT, Isaac - Huntington Twp., farmer, weak. Wife: Martha; children: Isaac, John, Elizabeth PEARSON, Susannah CLEAVER, Martha PEARSON, Hannah UNDERWOOD; executors: son John, Isaac PEARSON, son-in-law; witnesses: Thomas THORNBURGH, Nicholas WIERMAN; written: 20 Aug 1799; probate: 29 Aug 1801; recorded: pg 79

EWING, Thomas - Franklin Twp. Wife: Jane; children: Margaret, Sarah, Jane; executors: wife and John EDIE; witnesses: Alexander CALDWELL, William EWING; written: 16 Sep 1807; probate: 9 Oct 1807; recorded: pg 437

FERGUS, Hugh - Cumberland Twp. Wife: Sarah; children: John, Agnes wife of Thomas MCCLELAND, Thomas, Samuel; executors: Joseph WALKER, Henry CLUTS, John FERGUS; witnesses: William W. PATTERSON, David BRYNS, Robert MCCURDY; written: 8 Aug 1804; probate: 18 Aug 1804; recorded: pg 243

WILL BOOK A

FERGUSON, William - Menallen Twp., weak. Wife: Gartrude; children: Jane LEMMEN, John, Martha REIKER, James, William; executors: John WRIGHT Sr., Samuel WRIGHT; witnesses: John WRIGHT Jr., Thomas HOLMES Jr.; written: 25 Mar 1801; probate: 25 May 1801; recorded: pg 70

FINLEY, Ellenor - Hamiltonban Twp., weak. Bequests to: William LINN, nieces Elizabeth IRWIN, Martha LINN; Margaret JOHNSTON; executor: William LINN; witnesses: Thomas WHITE, Samuel KNOX; written: 23 Sep 1803; probate: 6 Feb 1804; recorded: pg 223

FINLEY, William - Hamiltonban Twp., weak. Wife: Eleoner; children: Mary wife of John MARTIN, Michael, Margaret wife of David HUMPHREY, Andrew, Elizabeth wife of David BLYTH, Ann (deceased) wife of Robert CAMPBELL, Finley (deceased son), Susanna wife of Robert ROWAN; negro Hamilton to be freed at wife's death; executors: son Michael, David BLYTH, son-in-law; witnesses: William MCCLEAN, Thomas WHITE; written: 6 Jun 1794; probate: 18 Sep 1800; recorded: pg 39

FLECK, Peter - Huntington Twp., weak. Children: Catharine, Jacob, Mary, Peter, Elizabeth, Dorothy, George, Nicholas, John, Susannah; grandson: Thomas; executor: Thomas PILKINGTON; witnesses: John FERKES, Jacob JONES, James ROBIN-ETTE; written: 12 Jan 1806; probate: 22 Jan 1806; recorded: pg 332

FLETCHER, Charles - Cumberland Twp., sick. Wife: Esther; children: Edward, John, Elizabeth wife of Archibald IRVINE, Mary wife of Thomas BRACKEN, Robert, James, David, Jennet; executors: son Edward, David MOOR; witnesses: John FLETCHER, John RITTER, Alexander RUSSELL; written: 2 Apr 1802; probate: 15 May 1802; recorded: pg 129

FOSTER, John - Franklin Twp., merchant, weak. Wife: Jane; children: Rebecca, William McClean FOSTER; brother: Edward FOSTER; bequest to: Margaret JOHNSTON, William MCCLEAN Sr.; executors: Alexander COBEAN, James DOBBIN; witnesses: John GORLEY, James BOYER/Jonas BAYER, Andrew THOMPSON; written: 15 Aug 1807; probate: 29 Sep 1807; wife renounced 1 Oct 1807; recorded: pg 433

GAISEL, Leonhart - Conewago Twp., advanced in age. Children: Ann Eve (to receive Negro James), Philip, Maria wife of Jacob KUNKLE, Juliana wife of George GELVIX, Margaret, Catharina (deceased); granddaughter: Eve HINKLE; executors: daughter Ann Eve, Henry SLAGLE Jr.; witnesses: David and Andrew MELHORN, Henry J. SLAGLE; written: 29 Jul 1805; probate: 28 Oct 1805; recorded: pg 320

GALLAGHER, Patrick - Berwick Twp., advanced in age. Wife: Judit; children: James, John, Bernard, Catherina wife of Christian WAGGONER, Christina, Eliner, Mary wife of Michael GALLAGHER, Edward, Daniel; grandson: John of Daniel; bequest to: Rev. W. S. BERTZ, Conewago Chapel; executors: Paul MILLER, John SLAGLE Esq.; witnesses: Jacob SLAGLE, John SNYDER; written: 7 Jan 1806; probate: 24 Jul 1806; recorded: pg 358

GETZ, Martin - Berwick Twp., farmer, very sick. Son: Jacob, also executor; witnesses: Daniel LINGEFELTER, Tobias KEPNER; written: 14 Jan 1806; probate: 30 Jan 1806; recorded: pg 334

GIFFEN, Stephen - Straban Twp., wheelwright, weak. Wife: Ann; children: Ann, William, Ester, Isabela wife of James MCCREARY, Elizabeth, Stephen; grandson: Andrew of Stephen; executors: William MCPHERSON, William GILLILAND; witnesses: Henry HOKE, David SCOTT, Alexander RUSSELL; written: 18 Jun 1794; probate: 1 Mar 1803; recorded: pg 179

GILBERT, George - Menallen Twp., weak. Wife: Elisabeth; children: George, Barnhart, Catharine wife of Frederick HUFFMAN, Susana, Elizabeth, Sarah; executors: son George, brother Lenhart GILBERT; witnesses; Jacob GILBERT, James MCCONAUGHY, William GILLILAND; written: 17 Mar 1803; probate: 28 Apr 1803; recorded: pg 182

WILL BOOK A

GOURLEY, Zibiah - Liberty Twp., widow of Thomas, sick. Children: Moses, James, Thomas, John; daughter-in-law, Margaret, wife of Moses; executor: son Moses; witnesses: Michael BOSSERMAN, John MORROW; written: 30 Apr 1804; probate: 8 Aug 1804; recorded: pg 239

GRAFT, Philip - Straban Twp., weak. Sons: Philip, John; granddaughter: Hannah GRAFT of John; executors: sons Philip, John; witnesses: William WALKER, Richard BROWN, James MCDONALD; written: 17 Feb 1800; probate: 9 Jun 1800; recorded: pg 34

GRAYBELL, Joseph - Franklin Twp., sick. Wife: Mary; children: Joel, Michael, Joseph, Shem, Eve wife of John WEYER, Lydia wife of John SHRIVER, Hannah wife of Abraham ZOOSSERMAN, Mary, Elizabeth, Sarah; grandsons: David, Ephraim of Ephraim (deceased); executors: sons Shem, Joel; witnesses: James KERR, James ---, Alexander RUSSELL; written: 7 May 1802; probate: 20 Sep 1802; codicil: written 3 Jul 1802, witnessed by Emanuel ZIEGLER, Henry HOKE, Alexander RUSSELL; recorded: pg 146

GROSCOST, John - Berwick Twp., very sick. Wife: Christina; children: John, Jacob, Elizabeth, Susanna wife of Joseph LITTLE, Christina wife of John KNIGHT, Daniel, Mary (deceased) wife of John BOLL--; executors: son Daniel, Samuel BOWSER Sr.; witnesses: Richard KNIGHT, Henry STAUP, John SLAGLE; written: 23 Sep 1801; probate: 27 Oct 1801; recorded: pg 95

GROUP, Peter - Huntington Twp, feeble. Wife: not named; children: Philip, Nicholas, Ludwick, George, Mary, Rosanna; executors: sons Nicholas, Ludwick; witnesses: Arthur and Mary NICKLE, Daniel FLECK; written: 17 Jul 1803; probate: 2 May 1806; recorded: pg 352

GROVE, Christian - Berlin, Berwick Twp., yeoman, sick. Wife: Catharine; children: Jacob, Catharine wife of John BARE, George; executor: George BROWN; witnesses: John NAUGLE, John FLEGER/FLEAGER; written: 11 Dec 1801; probate: 2 Jul 1805; recorded: pg 304

GURLAY, Thomas - Liberty Twp., weak. Wife: Zibiah; children: Moses, Thomas, John, James; executors: David WILSON, Alexander COBEAN; witnesses: John MORROW, William COBEAN, William PROCTER; written: 27 May 1803; probate: 9 Jun 1803; recorded: pg 196

HALL, Elsie - Cumberland Twp., widow of Edward HALL, weak. Children: William, Jenny, Elisabetha, Mary Ester, Edward; grandchildren: Nancy HALL, William WILLIAMS; executors: William MCCLELLAN Esq., David EDIE; witnesses: John and Thomas LATTA, David MOORE; written: 15 Jun 1799; probate: 19 Jun 1801; recorded: pg 71

HAMMOND, Thomas - Tyrone Twp., weak. Wife: Ruth; mother: Mary HAMMOND; father: James HAMMOND (deceased); child: Elisabeth; executors: George WILLSON, Nathan MCGREW; witnesses: John WRIGHT, John WRIGHT Jr, Jacob KOCH; written: 6 May 1802; probate: 20 Sep 1802; recorded: pg 145

HEMLER, Anna Elisabeth - McSherrystown, Mt Pleasant Twp., widow of Christian HEMLER, sick. Children: Henry, Susanna OBOLD, Mary Catherine SINDORF, Cathrina GINDER, another unnamed daughter, Joseph; bequest to: Rev. BARDT, Conewago Chapel; executors: sons Henry and Joseph; witnesses: John SLAGLE, Nicholas GINTHER; written: 8 Nov 1804; probate: 2 Jan 1805; recorded: pg 274

HERMAN, Catharine - Berwick Twp., very sick. Bequest to: John HERMAN; executor: Valentine HOLLINGER; witnesses: Solomon TATE, George BROWN; written: 11 Aug 1804; probate: 1 Jan 1805; recorded: pg 273

HESS, Rachel - Huntington Twp., widow of Valentine HESS, ancient. Son: Isaac (and his wife Lovis); executor: Herman BLAESSER, who renounced; witnesses: Henry MYER, Andrew HARTMAN; son Isaac named administrator; written: 11 Feb 1802; probate: 6 Mar 1805; recorded: pg 295

WILL BOOK A

HOBAUGH, Michael - Huntington Twp., weak. Bequests to: 5 children of Jacob SMITH, to Widow Magdalene WALDEBENY, to Nicholas MILLER, to Widow Mary FLEUR; money in Virginia to two friends there: Widow WALDEBENY, Youst LINETUER; to children of George SMITH; executor: John LEAR/LEAV; witnesses: Nichlaus WIRTZ, John SMITH; written: 4 Mar 1807; probate: 3 Apr 1807; recorded: pg 401

HOFFMAN, Christian - Heidelberg Twp., weak. Wife: Catharina; children: Maria, Anna, Elizabeth, John; executors: wife and Peter STORM; witnesses: Joseph OBOLD, John Lorentz GUBERNATOR; written: 26 Oct 1801; probate: 2 Dec 1802; recorded: pg 172

HOWIE, David - Liberty Twp., weak. Daughter: Prudence HOWIE; siblings: Robert HOWIE, Sarah BIGHAM; nephew: Robert BIGHAM; executors: Isaac MOORE, James MAGINLY; witnesses: Robert MCCLEAVE, James FEGEN, Patrick MONEY; written: 8 Sep 1803; probate: 6 Oct 1803; recorded: pg 215

HUTCHESON, John - Hamiltonban Twp., ill 8 yrs. Bequest of 50 pounds to Rev. Alexander DOBBINS, minister of the Gospel, living near Gettysburg, to help the deficiencies of his -- unpaid, hard earned stipends; 100 pounds to the poor; remainder of estate to David BLYTHE, with whom he resided; executor: David BLYTHE; witnesses: James AGNEW Sr., Thomas MEREDITH; written: 16 Mar 1799; probate: 12 Aug 1800; recorded: pg 38

HUTTON, William - Menallen Twp., weak. Children: Levi, Abner, Joseph, Deborah wife of George HAMMOND, John, Susanna (deceased) wife of Henry WIERMAN; grandchildren: Susanna, Pricilla, Deborah, Harman and William WIERMAN, Susanna, Rachel, Nathan and William HUTTON of son John; executors: sons Levi and Abner; witnesses: George HEWITT, John and William DELAP; written: 21 Nov 1796; probate: 8 Sep 1801; recorded: pg 82

JENKINS, Frances - Franklin Twp., infirm. Children: Walter, Moses, Rebeckah wife of John MONEY, Fanny, wife of James PARKER, Margaret wife of John SHEKLY; granddaughter: Ann GAMBLE; executors: John SHEKLY, William MCPHERSON; witnesses: John SWENEY, George and William SHEKLY; written: 9 Feb 1802; probate: 31 Mar 1804; recorded: pg 227

JONES, Jacob - Huntington Twp., sick. Wife: Gartrude; children: Henry, Jane, Jacob, Sarah, Rachel; nephew: Abraham OCCER; executors: sons Henry, Jacob; witnesses: John DAY, Thomas PEARSON; written: 16 Apr 1806; probate: 25 Apr 1806; recorded: pg 347

JUDSON, Elnathan - no location, weak. Estate to executor: Roger WALES; witnesses: John BREDEN, James DOBBIN; written: 26 Apr 1804; probate: 25 Jun 1804; recorded: pg 238

KEAGY, Jacob - Conewago Twp. Witnesses certified that they were present on 6 Oct 1802 to hear Keagy orally bequeath to his wife, Susanna. Witnessed 9 Oct 1802 "on the same day as the said Jacob KAEGY was buried". Witnesses: John BYER, Abraham KAEGY; probate: 23 Oct 1802; admin: Abraham KAEGY, Henry SLAGLE; recorded: pg 151

KERR, John - Berwick Twp., yeoman, weak. Wife: Sarah; nephews: James and John KERR of William (deceased), Thomas NEELY, son of Sarah widow of Samuel NEELY; sisters: Elizabeth wife of Thomas GRAY, Jane wife of John GILLENAN, Mary DORSOUGH (deceased), Susannah wife of John NEELY; brother-in-law: John DOUGLASS; sister-in-law: Agness, widow of John HUSTON; bequests to: Jane widow of Hugh CALDWELL, her son William HALL and to her unnamed children by CALDWELL, Sarah wife of James MCMASTER, Mary GROSCROST wife of William STURGEON, Alexander GROSCROST; executors: Andrew MCELWANE, Henry STURGEON Jr.; witnesses: Robert Johnston CHESTER/Richard CHESTER, Jacob and Christian KERBAUGH; written: 8 Dec 1786; probate: 26 Aug 1801; recorded: pg 66

KERR, Mary - Mt Pleasant Twp., widow of Josias KERR, weak. Children:

WILL BOOK A

Susannah COULTER, William KERR; executor: son William; witnesses: Robert MCILHINNY, Adam MORNINGSTAR; written: 10 Mar 1800; probate: 2 Apr 1804; recorded: pg 258

KERR, Sarah - no location, spinster, weak. Bequests to Jean SMYTH, daughter of sister Margaret MCINTIRE, to Mary GROSCORT, wife of William STURGEON; executors: Samuel SMYTH, William STURGEON; witnesses: George MCINTIRE, John STURGEON, Samuel SMYTH; written: 8 Apr 1804; probate: 16 Apr 1804; recorded: pg 228

KING, John - Tyrone Twp., very sick. Children: Agnes KING, Victor KING; executors: son Victor, brother Hugh KING; witnesses: William MCGREW, Richard BROWN, Victor KING son of Hugh; written: 11 Oct 1805; probate: 29 Oct 1805; recorded: pg 323

KING, Michael - Reading Twp. Wife: Margaret; children: Christian, Isaiah, Abraham, Susanna wife of John SKIDMORE, Nicholas, Margaret wife of Henry PICKING, Michael, Mary wife of Samuel TRUMP(?), Justina wife of Daniel MELOWN; grandson: John BURNS; executors: sons Christian and Michael; Christian renounced; witnesses: William MELOWN, William PATTERSON; written: 25 May 1801; probate: 19 Nov 1801; recorded: pg 97

KISSINGER, John - Cumberland Twp., weak. Wife: mentioned; children: John, Mary wife of John SMITH, Christiana wife of Dr. John DADY, David, Susanna, Louisa widow of Rice WILLIAMS, Abraham, David, Catharine wife of -- SHITZ, Jacob, Sophia wife of Joseph THOMPSON, Elizabeth wife of John BLACK; executors: son David, son-in-law John BLACK (renounced); witnesses: Peter WICKERT, Christian ROUTZONG, Alexander RUSSELL; written: 1 Feb 1805; probate: 21 Jun 1806; recorded: pg 354

KOHLSTOCK, John - Petersburgh, Germany Twp., weak. Wife: Mary; children: all underage; executor: wife, brother Henry KOHLSTOCK; witnesses: Robert MCILHINNY, Adam WINTRODE Jr.; wife renounced; written: 20 Nov 1801; probate: 16 Feb 1802; recorded: pg 167

KOLB, Valentine - Berwick Twp. Wife: Christiana; children: Cathrina, Eva, Susanna, Mary, Christiana, John; executors: wife and son; witnesses: Andrew MCELWAIN, William SMYTH, --BAILEY; written: 3 Jun 1802; probate: 23 Aug 1802; recorded: pg 138

KUNTZ, Andrew - Germany Twp., blacksmith, sick. Wife: Catharine; children: John, others mentioned; executors: Solomon MENCHEY, Michael KESSLER; witnesses: Robert MCILHINNY, Andrew HARTZIGER; written: 18 Aug 1804; probate: 21 Sep 1804; recorded: pg 250

KUPSER, Jacob - McSherrystown, Conewago Twp., weakly. Wife: Christina; bequest to Roman Catholic Church, Conewago; executor: wife; witnesses: Michael and Samuel KRAFT, John L. GUBERNATOR; name COOPSER in Conewago Church records; written: 1 Mar 1806; probate: 28 Oct 1806; recorded: pg 363

LANG, William - Straban Twp., yeoman, weak. Wife: Jean to receive Negro woman Lid; children: William (Negro man Furtune), Alexander (Negro woman Rue), Agness wife of Nathen WALKER, Gerrid; grandson: William WALKER; executors: sons Gerrid, William, Alexander; witnesses: Thomas NEELLE, William CASHMAN, William GILLILAND; written: 23 Oct 1801; probate: 25 Mar 1806; recorded: pg 341

LAUMAN, George - no location, sick. Also LOWMAN. Wife: Mary; children: George, Ephraim, Mary LOVE, Rebecca, Sarah LIGHT, Catharine, Susanna; stepson: John LAUMAN; executor: son George; witnesses: Thomas MCKEE, Abraham KREISS, Christian SMITH; written: 28 Oct 1800; probate: 25 Nov 1800; recorded: pg 52

LECKEY, Margaret - Mt Pleasant Twp., sick. Sisters: Serah MINTIETH, Catharine and Mary LECKEY, Isabella BARR; nieces: Elisabeth, Jenne, Serah MINTIETH; executor: James BARR; witnesses: Jacob HENCE, Gerrit DEMAREE, Jacob

WILL BOOK A

???; written: 20 Jan 1805; probate: 19 Mar 1805; recorded: pg 289
LILLY, Joseph - Conewago Twp., very sick. Wife: Sarrah; brother: John, his wife Mary and their sons, Henry and Samuel; bequest to Lewis BART of Conewago Church; executors: wife and nephew, Samuel LILLY; witnesses: Jacob KITZMILLER, John HEGI, Jacob ADAMS; written: 30 Jul 1804; probate: 18 Aug 1804; recorded: pg 241
LILLY, Thomas - Berwick Twp., somewhat indisposed. Late father: Samuel LILLY; brother: Joseph; nephews: Dudley DIGGES, Henry LILLY, Samuel LILLY of John; niece; Ann DIGGES; lot in Frederick, Md. to heirs of deceased sister, Mary BROWN; executors: nephews, Dudley DIGGES, Henry LILLY; witnesses: Henry SLAGLE, Henry WELSH, Paul METZGER; written: 16 Sep 1799; probate: 19 Oct 1804; recorded: pg 260
LINGAFELTER, Jacob - Berwick Twp., advanced in years. Children: Eve wife of Ulrich HOOVER, Elizabeth wife of Philip HULL, Catherina wife of George KERBAUGH, Ann Mary wife of John HULL, John, Jacob, Daniel (wife mentioned), unnamed daughter wife of Michael WOLLETT, Nicholas; executor: John SLAGLE; witnesses: Samuel BOUSER, Richard KITCHEN; written: 7 Jul 1807; probate: 18 Sep 1807; recorded: pg 424
LONG, Adam - Berwick Twp., weak. Wife: Susanna; children: Peter, Ann, Catharine, Teresa, Mary wife of George SHULTZ, executors: son Peter, Francis MARSHALL; witnesses: John and Nicholas MARSHALL, John GRIM; written: 15 Oct 1802; probate: 24 Nov 1802; recorded: pg 158
MARSHALL, James - Hamiltonban Twp. Wife: Elizabeth; children: Andrew, John, James, Samuel, Jane wife of John MCMUMM, Elizabeth; executors: wife and son Andrew; witnesses: Henry HOKE, James GETTYS, Alexander RUSSELL; written: 20 Sep 1803; probate: 5 Mar 1805; recorded: pg 285
MCALISTER, Alexander - Taneytown, Frederick Co., Md., weak. Wife: Margaret; children: John, James, Ginny, Polly KEN(?), Agness WILSON, Margaret HORNER, Sally ???; executors: son John, son-in-law James MCILHINNY; witnesses: Josiah KERN, John ADAIR, Thomas ESSOM; written: 26 Jun 1806; probate: 30 Apr 1807; recorded: pg 410
MCCLEAN, William - Carrols Tract, weak. Children: Mary, Ann, Sarah, Jane, John, William, James; mulatto slave Benn to be freed; servant Michael HANLEY; executors: son John, son-in-law James JOHNSTON; witnesses: John AGNEW, Moses MCCLEAN (certified will from Ross Co., Ohio); written: 23 Sep 1786; probate: 20 Oct 1807; recorded: pg 440
MCCLEARY, Elizabeth - Hamiltonban Twp. Bequest to Margaret, wife of James MCCLEARY; James, John, Joseph and Mary MCCLEARY of brother John (deceased); brother James MCCLEARY (deceased); executor: nephew James MCCLEARY; witnesses: William MILLER, John MCGINLEY, David MCCLELLAN; written: 20 Feb 1806; probate: 25 Apr 1806; recorded: pg 350
MCCLEARY, Michael - Hamiltonban Twp. Bequest to sister, Margaret MCCLELLAN; William and David MCCLEARY; niece Jean MCCLELLAN, wife of Joseph MCCLEARY; executors: Jacob MCCLELLAN Sr., William MILLER; witnesses: John and James REID, Michael MCCLELLAN; written: 5 May 1802; probate: 25 May 1802; recorded: pg 133
MCCONAUGHY, Samuel - Menallen Twp., yeoman, weak. Wife: Jean; children: Robert, John, Jean wife of Alexander HUNTER, Elizabeth wife of Robert RIDDLE, Sarah wife of Williamp THOMPSON, Margaret wife of David STEWART, Mary wife of Richard BLEAR, Jenney wife of Joseph BLEAR, Samuel (his wife Polly); granddaughter: Jean GLASGOW, daughter of Ann MCCONAUGHY; executors: David MOORE, William GILLILAND; witnesses: William LAIRD, Robert GRAHAM, Samuel GILLILAND; written: 2 Dec 1801; probate: 24 Apr 1802; recorded: pg 123

WILL BOOK A

MCCRAKEN, Alexander - Liberty Twp., weak. Daughters: Margaret, Nancy; son-in-law, William PORTER; grandson: Alexander MARTIN; executors: Thomas MCKEE, Isaac MOORE; witnesses: Robert HOWIE, John BEARD, Patrick MONEY; written: 5 Jun 1803; probate: 18 Jun 1803; recorded: pg 201

MCGAUGHY, Agness - Hamiltonban Twp., sick. Children: James, Agness CARNOHAN, Ann SCOTT, Alexander; daughter-in-law: Anne MCGAUGHY; granddaughters: Agness McKean SCOTT, Agnes of son James; executor: son James; witnesses: Thomas WHITE, John KERR; written: 23 Sep 1804; probate: 27 Nov 1804; recorded: pg 264

MCGINLEY, Patrick - Berwick Twp., weak. Wife: Mary; daughters: Margaret, Nancy; executor: Henry KUHN, renounced; administrator: Nicholas MARSHALL; witnesses: William STURGEON, Bastian WEISS; written: 22 Feb 1796; probate: 9 Jun 1803; recorded: pg 198

MCGLAUGHLIN, James - Franklin Twp., weak. Bequest to: Ketty and Mary, of brother Jeremiah of Kingdom of Ireland; James MCCONOMY, of sister Ketty MCCONOMY, of Ireland; Francis, John, Rosey and Ketty of brother Francis of Ireland; tombstones to be placed on his grave, his late wife, and nephew James MCGLAUGHLIN; executors: Peter MARK, Alexander COBEAN; witnesses: John and Daniel MECKLY; written: 13 Apr 1803; probate: 19 May 1803; recorded: pg 190

MCGRAIEL, Owen - Menallen Twp., sick. Children: George, Mary wife of Nathan HENDRICKS, Sarah wife of John HUTTON; grandchildren: Mary MCKNICKLE, Sarah and Mary MCGRAIEL of John (deceased); Elizabeth and Lydia MCGRAIEL, widows of sons James and William; executors: son George, George HEWITT; witnesses: John and William DELAP, Peter PUFFENBERGER; written: 20 Dec 1799; probate: 11 May 1802; recorded: pg 127

MCGREW, Archibald Sr. - Huntington Twp. WIfe: Martha; sons: John, Archabald; grandchildren: Archabald, Jean of John; Archabald, Eave FLATCHER of John FLATCHER; Archabald, Mary of Archabald; Archabald, Mary of son-in-law Alexander MCGREW; James, Weakly, Martha, Jean, Elisa, Maria of William (deceased); Margaret, Martha, Mary of son-in-law Moses CARSON; Cathrina, Esther, William of son-in-law John BOYD; executors: sons John, Archabald; witnesses: Matthew DILL, Andrew RALSTON, John MCGREW Jr.; written: 13 May 1802; probate: 27 Feb 1805; recorded: pg 291

MCMURDY, Robert - Adams County, weak. Siblings: Isaac, Martha; executor: Henry CLUTS (landlord); witnesses: William W. PATTERSON, William DONALDSON, Martin CLUTS; written: 11 Nov 1806; probate: 10 Dec 1806; recorded: pg 367

MCPHERSON, Agness - Cumberland Twp., widow. Children: Jennet GRIER, Mary RUSSELL, Agness MCDOWEL, William (his wife Sarah), John; grandchildren: Agness, Mary, Jane and Peggy GRIER, Agness and Alexander RUSSELL, Agness Miller MCDOWEL, Agness and Elisa RIDDLE, Polly MCPHERSON; Negro servant Nanny to be freed; executors: sons-in-law Alexander RUSSELL, Andrew MCDOWEL, James RIDDLE; witnesses: James and Thomas SWENEY, David EDIE; written: 8 May 1802; probate: 16 Sep 1802; recorded: pg 141

MCQUIN, Isaabella - Menallen Twp., weak. Children: James, Frederick, Archy RIED, Deborah wife of John MCCLEY; nephew: Robert HAMILTON; executor: John MCCLEY, son-in-law; witnesses: Samuel WILLSON, Robert BARRON; written: 26 Aug 1803; probate: 11 Feb 1804; recorded: pg 226

MESSERSMITH, George - Adams County. Bequest to: Philip SMITH and wife, --- ELEY and wife, Henry DEWOLT and wife; Mrs SMITH is brother's daughter, ELEY'S wife is 'my wife's brother's daughter'; executors: Christian HAGST, Philip SMITH; witnesses: Daniel BAKER, Jacob MESHLER, John JOHN(?); written: 18 Feb 1803; probate: 10 Mar 1803; recorded: pg 181

MILLER, Nicholas - Mt Joy Twp., weak. Wife: Barbara; children: Ludwick, Margaret wife of John KUNTZ, other children; grandsons: John HAUPTMAN, John

WILL BOOK A

KUNTZ; executors: son Ludwick, brother-in-law Jacob PARR; witnesses: Robert MCILHINNY, Samuel HUNTER, Jacob ACKER; written: 20 Mar 1804; probate: 19 May 1804; recorded: pg 235
    MOORE, David - Cumberland Twp., weak. Wife: Elisabeth; children: Joseph, William, David (three in Virginia), Patrick (land in Westmoreland Co.), Archibald, John, Robert, Moses, Thomas; granddaughter: Eliza Wright MOORE of Samuel (deceased); bequest to Rev. David MCCONAUGHY, Upper Presbyterian congregation of Marshcreek; executors: sons Patrick, David; witnesses: William WILSON, William MCGAUGHEY, Alexander RUSSELL; written: 17 Jun 1803; probate: 25 Jun 1803; recorded: pg 203
    MOORE, James - Huntington Twp., weak. Children: William, James, Agnes; brothers William and John MOORE, and James MOORE Esq to be guardians of William; executors: brothers William and John MOORE, James MOORE Esq. of Cumberland Co., Pa., son James, son-in-law Ludwick WALTEMYRE; witnesses: James WILSON, William GRAHAM; written: 19 May 1802; codicil: 11 Dec 1804 witnessed by Peter GRUPE, John THOMPSON Sr.; probate: 28 Jan 1805; recorded: pg 279
    MURRET, Michael - Straban Twp., yeoman, weak (also MURRAT). Wife: Margaret; children: Peter, Barbara, Michael, John, Jacob, Nicholas, all minors; executors: brother Peter MURRET, Jacob WERTS; witnesses: Jacob MAY, William GILLILAND; written: 2 Feb 1802; probate: 23 Feb 1802; recorded: pg 109
    MYER, Barbara - Berwick Twp., widow, very sick. Children: Elizabeth wife of Charles REINHARD, Jacob, John; grandchildren: John and ELizabeth STRIETH; executor: Christopher HOLLINGER; witnesses: George SPANGLER, Tobias KEPNER; written: 12 Feb 1804; probate: 8 Dec 1804; recorded: pg 271
    MYERS, David - Berlin town. Wife: Mary; daughter: Peggy wife of Peter BINDER; grandchildren: Nancy and David JAMESON; executors: brother Jacob MYERS, Frederick ASPER; witnesses: John ATTIG, William PATTERSON; written: 27 Oct 1805; probate: 26 Nov 1805; recorded: pg 329
    MYERS, Frederick - Berwick Twp. Wife: Margaret; children: Peter, Jacob, Frederick, Adam, Catharina wife of Jacob RIFF, Elizabeth wife of Peter HOKE, Eve; land in Frederick Co., Md.; executors: sons Frederick, Adam; witnesses: George BARDT, Peter KEPLINGER, Joseph MARSHALL; written: 3 Sep 1804; probate: 26 Jan 1807; recorded: pg 369
    MYERS, Martin - Liberty Twp., sick. Wife: Barbara; children: Mary, John, Jacob, Martin, David and unnamed daughter, all minors; executors: Mathias WINEBRIGHT, Peter WICART; witnesses: William BIGHAM, James MCKINLEY; written: 6 Aug 1804; probate: 14 Sep 1804; recorded: pg 244
    NEELY, John - Reading Twp., yeoman, weak. Wife: Susana; children: James, Thomas, Jonathan, John, Agness MCCURDY, Sarah wife of William POTTER, Elizabeth wife of John GRAFT, Susana wife of George WHITE; granddaughter: Marthew NEELY; executors: son Thomas, Anthony DEARDUFF aka Little Anthony DEARDUFF; witnesses: Daniel SLAGLE, William MCFARLAND, William GILLILAND; written: 2 Apr 1801; probate: 12 Oct 1801; recorded: pg 87
    NICKEL, James - Huntington Twp., weak. Wife: Sarah; children: Mary, David, John, Robert, James, William, Arthur, Elizabeth BALES, Rebekah RICHIE, Sarah WIERMAN, Hannah STEPHENS, Susannah PETENTURPH; executors: wife and son John; witnesses: Nicholas GROOP, John SADLER; written: 17 Oct 1803; probate: 29 Dec 1803; recorded: pg 220
    OBIS, John - Heidleberg Twp., "on my bed very sick". Estate to Conewago Church; executor: Jacob ADAMS; witnesses: John KUHNS, Richard ADAMS; written: 21 Apr 1800; probate: 2 Jun 1800; recorded: pg 30
    O'BLENIS, John - Reading Twp., weak. Wife: Mary; children: Sarah wife of James NEELY, Daniel, Elizabeth "who was married to" Isaac WILSON, John, Barbara, Peter, Polly; land in Cayuga Co., N.Y.; executors: Daniel SLAGLE,

WILL BOOK A

Christian BUSHY (renounced), William PATTERSON; witnesses: Simon BECHER, John B. ARNOLD; written: 9 Oct 1805; probate: 19 Oct 1805; recorded: pg 316
OBOLT, Sebastian - Heidleberg Twp., advanced in age, weak. Children: Joseph, Antony, Elizabeth wife of Paul MILLER, Mary wife of Antony SHORROP; grandchildren: Mary, Elizabeth and John of Joseph's first wife; executors: son Joseph, Casper WISE; witnesses: Nicholas WALTER, Andrew SMITH, Henry SLAGLE; written: 28 Mar 1800; probate: 1 Apr 1800; recorded: pg 6
OYLER, Jacob - Menallen Twp., weak. Wife: Barbara; children: Jacob, Michael, Susana, Valentine, Elizabeth, Sarah, Barbara, Daniel, Mary wife of Daniel BECHDOL; stepmother mentioned; executors: son Michael, George HICKENLUBER; witnesses: John REISS, John NEELY, Thomas COCHRAN; written: 9 Jul 1807; probate: 28 Jul 1807; recorded: pg 414
PEDAN, Samuel - Liberty Twp., weak. Children: Elizabeth wife of John RAMSEY, Greesy (Grace?), Rebekah BOUGLE, John, Sarah, Susanah; son-in-law, James WHITE; grandchildren: Elizabeth and Samuel WHITE, Samuel, Thomas and Elizabeth RAMSEY, Samuel BOUGLE; tombstones to be placed at graves of himself, wife, and deceased daughter Mary WHITE; executors: son John, Andrew REED; witnesses: John ZIMMERMAN, John AGNEW, Samuel MCNAIR; written: 1 Aug 1802; probate: 6 Sep 1802; recorded: pg 139
PELLENTZ, James - Hidelberg Twp., Roman Catholic priest, weak. Bequest to Francis Xavier BROSIUS, priest, including land in Rye Twp., Cumberland Co., Pa.; executor: BROSIUS; witnesses: Joseph LILLY, James DRISKELL, Jacob KUHN; written: 14 Jun 1795; probate: 23 Apr 1800; recorded: pg 16
POLLOCK, William - Menallen Twp., weak. Siblings: Joseph (deceased), Elenor wife of John STOCKTON, Rachel wife of George BLANKLEY, Mary wife of Robert MCGARVEY; nieces: Catharine, Mary, Elisabeth POLLOCK, Mary STOCKTON; sister-in-law: Mary POLLOCK, wife of Joseph; executor: William GILLILAND; witnesses: Adam WALTER, Robert BARRON; written: 6 Apr 1802; probate: 29 Jun 1802; recorded: pg 135
PORTER, Samuel - Hamiltonban Twp. Daughter: Jane wife of William CLERK, Fayette Co., Pa.; grandchildren: John MCCREA, Samuel Alexander CLERK; nephew: Samuel PORTER (and his son Samuel); Samuel MCCLEAN named guardian of Samuel A. CLERK; executor: Mosses MCCLEAN; witnesses: John and William MCCLEAN; written: 1 Oct 1797; probate: 16 Apr 1800; recorded: pg 10
PORTER, William - Liberty Twp., weak. Wife: Sarah; children: Jeremiah, Richard, Elizabeth RAMSEY, James, Nathaniel, William, Elenor PATTERSON; furniture to Betsey RAMSEY, Ales FLEMIN; Negros Rose and Heney (little girl) to wife; executors: sons Jeremiah and Richard; witnesses: William MCMILLEN, John HILL; written: 30 Apr 1803; probate: 5 May 1803; recorded: pg 188
PROCTER, John - Huntington Twp., weak. Wife: Sarah; children: John, Levi, Abner, Rachel, Sinclear, Sarah COPPERSTONE, Richard, Joanna; granddaughter: Ruth PROCTER 'daughter to Sarah COPPERSTONE'; executors: son John, Edward HATTAN; witnesses: James HATTON, Daniel FLECK, Daniel BOWER; written: 25 Sep 1806; probate: 11 Oct 1806; recorded: pg 361
RECK, Christian - Cumberland Twp., sick. Wife: Sophia; children: John, Elizabeth wife of Abraham LIGHTEWALTER Jr., Jacob, Catherine, Christian, Sarah, Samuel, William, David; executors: wife, son John, Samuel RECKER; witnesses: Henry CLUTZ, Jacob MEARING, Alexander RUSSELL; written: 12 Mar 1807; probate: 22 Apr 1807; recorded: pg 404
REID, James - Hamiltonban Twp. Wife: Margaret; children: Mary wife of James STEVENSON, Benjamin, John, Sarah wife of William MCKESSON, William, Thomas, Samuel; daughter-in-law: Mary wife of John; executors: wife and son John (John surviving executor at probate); witnesses: James BRICE, James REID;

11

WILL BOOK A

BRICE confirmed will in Pittsburgh, Pa. 13 Feb 1804; written: 7 Dec 1796; probate: 26 Jan 1803; recorded: pg 177

REYNOLDS, William - Mt Pleasant Twp., yeoman, weak. Children: Sarah wife of Josiah KERR, William, Joseph, John; sister: Mary SOOTER (?); executor: son John, renounced; William KERR appointed administrator; witnesses: Joseph and James THOMPSON, John PATTON; written: 1 Jul 1795; probate: 13 Feb 1802; recorded: pg 163

RIFFLE, Jinny - Mt Joy Twp., widow of Mathias RIFFLE, weak. Children: Joseph, Melchor, George; executor: son Joseph; witnesses: Samuel HUNTER, Henry STOLTZ; written: 24 Dec 1800; probate: 7 Feb 1801; recorded: pg 60

RUSSELL, James - Franklin Twp., weak. Wife: Hannah; children: Samuel, Alexander, John (deceased), James, Mary wife of Acheson LAUGHLIN, Elizabeth wife of James SPEER, Hannah wife of David HOSACK, Jennet wife of John DICKSON; grandsons: James McPherson RUSSELL of Alexander, James RUSSELL of John; executors: sons Samuel and Alexander; witnesses: James COBEAN, Archibald FLETCHER, Matthew BLACK; written: 19 Mar 1804; probate: 9 May 1804; recorded: pg 231

RUSSELL, Jean - Franklin Twp., widow of Joshua RUSSELL, sick. Granddaughters: Jenny, Mary, Rachel and Margaret Eliza RUSSELL; executor: nephew Alexander RUSSELL; witnesses: Francis MCNUTT, John LAIRD; written: 5 Jan 1807; probate: 28 Jan 1807; recorded: pg 379

RUSSELL, John - Franklin Twp., very sick. Wife: Sarah; children: Joseph, Elisa, James, Rachel; executors: wife, brother Alexander RUSSELL; witnesses: James, Samuel and Mary RUSSELL; written: 18 Jan 1802; probate: 20 Sep 1802; recorded: pg 143

RUSSELL, Samuel - Franklin Twp., very sick. Father: Joshua RUSSELL (deceased); wife: Jenny; children: Jenny, Molly, Rachel and unborn child (see RUSSELL, Jean above); Negros Betsey, to mother, Jam and Dinah to wife; executors: wife, cousin Alexander RUSSELL; witnesses: John LAIRD, John ROSS, Michael BENNEDICT; written: 24 Jan 1806; probate: 1 Feb 1806; recorded: pg 335

SANDERSON, Alexander - Huntington Twp. Wife: Elizabeth; children: John, James, Mary NEESBIT, Thomas, Samuel, Elizabeth wife of Joshua PORTER; executors: son John, George ROBINETTE; witnesses: John and Thomas BONNER, Stephen FOULK Jr.; written: 12 Nov 1800; probate: 12 Jan 1801; recorded: pg 55

SAUM, Mathias - Menallen Twp., yeoman, very sick. Wife: Madlena; children: Mathias, Jacob, Madlena, Catharina, Susannah, Elizabeth, Barbara; executors: Henry SLEBAUGH, Thomas COCHRAN; witnesses: Mary SLEBAUGH, George THOMAS, Philip HARTZEL; written: 17 Jan 1804; probate: 26 Apr 1804; recorded: pg 229

SCHRIVER, Ludwick - Conewago Twp., very sick. Wife: Magdalena; five children including Cathrina wife of Daniel COBRIGHT, Samuel; executors: Daniel COBRIGHT, Jacob ADAMS; witnesses: John MILLER, Jacob SHULTZ; written: 13 Sep 1804; probate: 8 Oct 1804; recorded: pg 257

SNEERINGER, John - Conewago Twp., yeoman, very sick. Wife: Juliana; children: Lawrence, Catharina (deceased) wife of Christian ECKENROTH, Christina wife of Jacob SHORB, Margaretha wife of Adam KEHLENBERGER, John; daughter Catharina left six children, three raised by decedent, three by Henry ECKENROTH of Donagall; executors: son John, son-in-law Adam KEHLENBERGER; witnesses: Henry GRAFT, J. L. GUBERNATOR, Lorentz SNEERINGER; written: 23 Apr 1804; probate: 16 May 1804; recorded: pg 233

SNEERINGER, Lorrantz - Mt Pleasant Twp., weak. Wife: Catharine; children: John, Peter, others; executors: Joseph KUHN, Adam KILLENBERGER; witnesses: Robert MCILHINNY, Dennis COLLINS, John MCSHERRY; written: 10 Nov 1804; probate: 7 Jan 1804; recorded: pg 276

WILL BOOK A

SPEAKMAN, Joshua - Huntington Twp. Children: Stephen, Ebenezer, Thomas, Hannah wife of Thomas SHOPTON, Susanna wife of Jacob COOK, Joanna wife of Robert SQUIBB, Phebe wife of Robert ????, James; grandchildren: Willis, Elizabeth, James of James; executors: son Stephen, Allen ROBBINET; witnesses: Elihu UNDERWOOD, Thomas MCCREARY; written: Sep 1801 (no day); probate: 7 Jan 1802; recorded: pg 105

STANLEY, John - Franklin Twp., farmer, advanced in age. Wife: Hanna; children: James, William, Martha MOORHEAD, Mary MOORHEAD, Rebeckah; bequest to Rebeckah's child if it lives; executors: son William, Peter MARK, miller; witnesses: John and Robert CRISWELL, Benjamin WORKMAN; written: no date; probate: 3 Oct 1807; recorded: pg 431

STEWART, Mary - formerly of Hamiltonban Twp., now of Liberty Twp., widow of James STEWART. Children: William, Elizabeth wife of Thomas ADAMS, Andrew; grandson: James of Andrew; executor: son Andrew; witnesses: James MOORE, Joseph WALKER, Alexander RUSSELL; written: 2 Aug 1805; probate: 6 Feb 1807; recorded: pg 381

STEWART, Robert Sr. - Adams County, weak. Wife: Agness; children: James, Elizabeth wife of David BRINES, Robert; grandson: Samuel STEWART; executors: wife, James and Robert STEWART; witnesses: William ADAIR, James STEWART Sr., Michael ZEYER; written: 15 Sep 1801; probate: 24 Dec 1801; recorded: pg 103

STIVISON, George - Huntington Twp. Wife: Elizabeth; children: Barny, Joan, John, William (all minors); executors: John LEESE, Burkhard WARDNER; witnesses: Jacob MONTORF, Henry FISSEL, Philip EBBERT; written: 7 Mar 1806; probate: 23 Feb 1807; recorded: pg 385

STOCKSLEGAR, Joseph - Mt Joy Twp., weak. Wife: Elizabeth; children: Nancy, Frederick, John, Joseph, Elizabeth; executors: brother-in-law Abraham STONER, Jacob MUNDORFF; witnesses: Frederick STONER, Henry STOLTZ, Alexander RUSSELL; written: 23 Jun 1801; probate: 1 Aug 1801; recorded: pg 75

STOCKSLEGAR, Nancy - Franklin Twp., widow, weak. Children: John, Barbara wife of Christian THOMAS, Nancy wife of Mathias ZACHARIAS, Betsey wife of Isaac BYERS, Joseph (deceased), Mary, Susan, Albertus; executors: Jacob SHANK, Andrew HANSLEMAN; witnesses: Alexander COBEAN, Alexander RUSSELL; written: 28 Apr 1802; probate: 2 May 1803; recorded: pg 187

STUMP, George Adam - Cumberland Twp. Wife: Sarah; son: Jess(?), now an infant; executor: Matthias COPLIN; witnesses: Jacob HARPER, Joseph THOMPSON; written: 15 Oct 1801; probate: 18 Oct 1801; recorded: pg 90

SUTTLE, Conrad - Franklin Twp., yeoman. Wife: Mary; children: William, Henry, Jacob, Becky wife of Peter WION, Elizabeth wife of George WALTER, Ann wife of William SLAYBAUG, Sarah wife of Henry TOOT, Catherine wife of Valentine FLOAR, Peter; grandson: John ARNDT; executors: Jacob GREENEMYER, Nicholas MARKS; witnesses: William MCCLEAN, William MCCLEAN Jr., Mosses MCCLEAN; written: 13 Feb 1800; probate: 20 Sep 1803; recorded: pg 213

WALTER, Nicholas - McSherrystown, school master, old and sick. Wife: Rosanna; children: Maryan, Nicholas Peter, John; bequest to Barbara GINDER, 3 children of son John; executor: Peter SHENFELTER; witnesses: Jacob TRINE, Nicholas GINTHER; written: 15 Sep 1804; probate: 27 Oct 1804; recorded: pg 263

WATSON, William - Mt Pleasant Twp., old and infirm. Children: Jennet SWAN, John, Aaron, Patrick, Hugh, Sarah, Catharine, Mary, Rebecca; bequest to eldest sons of Jennet, John and Patrick; executors: son Hugh, nephew Alexander LECKEY; witnesses: Joseph WILSON, Aaron TORRENCE, William EWING; written: 31 May 1799; probate: 20 Nov 1802; recorded: pg 157

WEAVER, Conrad - Part of Managhan Twp., ancient and sick. Children: Anna KIMMEL, Elizabeth KIMMEL, Salomeneo MEYER, Conrad; executor: son Conrad;

witnesses: James KENNEDY, William GODFREY Jr., Francis COULSON; written: 10 Aug 1803; probate: 17 Feb 1807; recorded: pg 383

WEAVER, Henry - Cumberland Twp., infirm. Wife: Elizabeth; children: Barbara wife of Christian STAUFFER, Henry, Jacob, John, George, David, Samuel, Joseph, Elizabeth, Benjamin, Peter; executors: wife and sons, Samuel and Joseph; witnesses: Patrick HAGEN, Alexander RUSSELL, Abraham LIGHTENWALLEN; written: 6 Jun 1807; probate: 11 Sep 1807; recorded: pg 421

WERTS, Jacob - Straban Twp., yeoman, weak. Wife: Cristena; children: Jacob, Burk, Michael, George, John, Cristena wife of John SLUSSER, Catharine wife of Peter RUFFELSBARGER, Barbara wife of Peter BERGER, Margaret wife of George RUDISELL, Susana wife of Nicholas DETRICK; executors: sons Jacob and Burk; witnesses: George EYSTER, William GILLILAND; written: 30 Sep 1805; probate: 18 Oct 1805; recorded: pg 312

WHITE, John - Tyrone Twp., weak. Children: Margaret wife of Thomas NEELY, James (received time of servant boy James LIGHTNER), Agness wife of Jacob G. LANG, Jean wife of William STEWART, Martha wife of James MCFINDLEY, Rebekah; executors: son James, James ELLIOTT, John MILEY Esq; witnesses: John B. ARNOLD, David POLLOCK, William PATTERSON; written: 4 Feb 1806; probate: 25 Feb 1806; recorded: pg 338

WHITLEY, Benjamin - Mt Pleasant Twp., weak. Wife: Jean; children: Andrew, Benjamin, William, Mary JOHNSTON, Elizabeth GRAFF, Rebeckah HUNTER; former son-in-law, John LONGWELL; grandchildren: Jean and Benjamin JOHNSTON, Jean GRAFF, Benjamin LONGWELL; executors: wife and sons Andrew and Benjamin; wife and Andrew renounced; witnesses: Garret VAN ARSDALIN, John MONFORT; written: 30 May 1805; probate: 17 Apr 1806; recorded: pg 344

WIEGHTNER, Abraham - Tyrone Twp., yeoman, sick. Wife: Mary; children: Jacob, William, Abraham, Susanna wife of John FLICK, Catharine; executors: sons John and William; witnesses: Nathan MCGREW, Henry SCHMEISER; written: 15 Jan 1807; probate: 29 Apr 1807; recorded: pg 406

WIERMAN, Henry - Huntington Twp. Wife: Elizabeth; children: Hannah MORGAN, William, Gratrude WORLEY, Samuel, John, Ann, Sarah, Mary COOK, Priscilla DILL, Catharine NEWLIN; grandchild: Elizabeth WORLEY; executors: son John, John WRIGHT; witnesses: Nicholas WIERMAN, Nicholas WIERMAN cordwinder, Thomas WIERMAN; written: 6 Oct 1807; probate: 9 Mar 1802; recorded: pg 111

WIERMAN, John Sr. - Huntington Twp., weak. Wife: Mary; children: Nicholas, Henry, Samuel, William, Eleanor HOWEL, Gertrude PENROSE, Mary HART, Catherine, Hannah, Rachel BEALS, Phebe, James, John; son-in-law: Nehemiah HOWEL; sons Henry and Samuel receive land at Possom Creek Settlement; executors: John FICKES, Thomas PEARSON; witnesses: William WIERMAN, Joseph GRIEST; written: 11 Jul 1804; probate: 18 Sep 1804; recorded: pg 246

WIERMAN, Sarah Sr. - Huntington Twp. Children: William, Benjamin, Phebe THORNBURGH, Nicholas; granddaughters: Sarah and Susanna of Nicholas; executors: son Nicholas, Andrew THOMPSON Esq.; witnesses: William WIERMAN Jr., Joseph GRIEST; written: 29 Dec 1800; probate: 29 Dec 1802; recorded: pg 175

WILLET, Jacob - Germany Twp., yeoman, "in my bed very sick". Wife: Rosana; 9 children including John; executors: wife, brother Anthony WILLET; witnesses: Jacob BIEHL, Frederick BALMER, Jacob ADAMS; written: 9 Oct 1806; probate: 25 Nov 1806; recorded: pg 365

WILLIAMS, Thomas - Menallen Twp. Wife: Jean; executors: wife, George HEWITT; witnesses: Joseph and John HEWITT, Anna LEECH; written: 3 Dec 1801; probate: 1 May 1807; recorded: pg 412

WILSON, William - Hamiltonban Twp., weak. Children: James, Jean, Polly CARSON, John; grandson: William WILSON; executors: son John, daughter Jean;

witnesses: Hugh and David WILSON, John AGNEW; written: 12 May 1803; probate: 19 Sep 1805; recorded: pg 310

WIREMAN, William - Huntington Twp., weak. Wife: Emy; children: William, Cathrine, Emy, Mary; executors: son William, kinsman Thomas THORNBURG; witnesses: Nicholas WEIRMAN, Thomas PENROSE, Thomas GRIEST; written: 20 Jun 1790; probate: 23 Apr 1802; recorded: pg 119

WISE, Casper Sr. - Berwick Twp., farmer, very sick. Wife: Catharine; children: Casper, Abraham, Catharine wife of Sebastian HICKLEY, Susanna wife of Anthony OBOLD, Elizabeth, Christina; executors: son Casper, Tobias KEPNER; written: 20 Dec 1802; codicil: 21 Dec 1802 bequest to Mr. BROSIUS, priest, at Roman Catholic Church; witnesses: John B. ARNOLD, John HOLLINGER, John SHULTZ; probate: 14 Dec 1803; recorded: pg 217

WOLF, Frederick Sr. - Berwick Twp., farmer, very sick. Wife: Susanna; children: Christina, Frederick, Elizabeth, Jacob, Mary, John, Andrew; executors: son John, son-in-law John NOLL, Henry HULL; witnesses: Frederick BAGHER, Tobias KEPNER; written: 17 Mar 1803; probate: 28 May 1803; recorded: pg 193

YOUNG, Peter - Mt Pleasant Twp., old and infirm. Children: Rachel WARHAM, Elizabeth DEITRICK (deceased), John, David (land in Frederick Co., Md.); grandsons: Samuel ESTER, John YOUNG of David; executor: son John; witnesses: Robert MCILHINNY, Christian FRIED; written: 23 Jun 1803; probate: 1 Sep 1803; recorded: pg 208

WILL BOOK B

ACKERMAN, Jacob - Gettysburg, sick. Wife: Catharine; children: Catharine wife of John TROXELL Jr., Mary wife of Valentine NEASWITZ, Rachel wife of George ROWE, Sarah, Rebeccah, Joshua; executors: wife, son-in-law John TROXELL Jr.; witnesses: Samuel KEPLINGER, John AGNEW, Alexander RUSSELL; written: 8 Nov 1808; probate: 14 Nov 1808; recorded: pg 25

ADAIR, William - Mt Joy Twp. Children: Hannah, Anna, Elizabeth wife of James PAXTON, Mary WILSON (deceased), John; grandchildren: Nathaniel and William PAXTON, two WILSON children; apprentice boy: William BEARD; executor: son John; witnesses: R. MCILHENNY, Samuel and John MCILHENNY; written: 18 Jun 1807; probate: 28 Feb 1810; recorded: pg 66

ADAMS, Richard - Conewago Twp., very sick. Wife: Margaret; children: Anna, Joseph, Jacob, Elisabeth, Mary Magdalen, Richard; executors: wife, Mathias MARTIN; witnesses: Ignatius and Jacob ADAMS; written: 18 Oct 1813; probate: 6 Nov 1813; recorded: pg 274

AGNEW, John - Hamiltonban Twp. Wife: Jane; bequests to: John Agnew SCOTT, son of Hugh SCOTT, John Agnew CUMMINS, son of --- CUMMINS, John AGNEW of John AGNEW (deceased); executors: Samuel MCCULLOUGH, Samuel WITHEROW; witnesses: Robert HAYES, John MCCONAUGHY; written: 6 Oct 1813; probate: 10 Jun 1814; recorded: pg 330

AKERMAN, Barbara - Tyrone Twp. Sister: Margaret MYERS, and her son Jacob MYERS, miller; executor: nephew Jacob MYERS; witnesses: Hugh KING, Henry MYERS, Moses FUNK; written: 17 May 1810; probate: 29 Jul 1811; recorded: pg 167

ASHBAUGH, Andrew - Mt Joy Twp., farmer, weak. Wife: Mary; children: mentioned; executors: son Thomas, son-in-law: Adam WINTERODE; witnesses: R. MCILHENNY, Robert WILSON, George BENDER(?); written: 25 Mar 1813; probate: 12 Mar 1814; recorded: pg 294

BAER, Philip Jacob - Franklin Twp. Wife: mentioned; mentions a first wife; 12 children including Jacob (eldest son), Nicholas, Peter (does not see well), Catherina, George, Henry, Elizabeth, Anamaria, John, eldest daughter blind); executors: son Jacob, Henry WALTER; witnesses: Peter HEIN, Mathias SAHN/SAUM; Jacob renounced, Nicholas named admin; will signed by legate, Susanna and Nicholas BAER; written: 1 Mar 1794; probate: 6 Oct 1804; recorded: pg 337

BAILEY, Mary Ann - Straban Twp., weak. Daughters: Margaret and Nancy, land in Sunbury and Philadelphia; executors: James and Alexander DOBBIN; witnesses: Joseph MCKILEP, Christinah CASSAT; written: 17 Aug 1814; probate: 23 Aug 1814; recorded: pg 334

BARR, James - Mt Joy Twp., weak and infirm. Wife: Isabella; children: Mary LEECH, Sarah, Nancy, Peggy, Alexander Lecking, George, James; executor: son James; witnesses: Robert and John HUNTER, Ehiel MCILHINNY; written: 3 Feb 1814; probate: 25 Nov 1814; recorded: pg 361

BEALS, Jacob - Latimore Twp., weak. Wife: Mary; siblings: Hannah HILLDEBRAND, John, Elizabeth FLETCHER, Rachel ----, Jonathan, Elisha, Leah WATSON, Mary GARRETT (eldest sister) and her son Luke GARRETT; bequests to Caleb, James and Stephen HILDEBRAND, sons of nephew James HILDEBRAND, and Mary wife of Jacob KINERD; executors: David GREIST, Jacob KINERD; witnesses: Caleb and Jacob BEALS, Caleb BEALS Jr.; written: 8 Dec 1812; probate: 5 Jan 1813; recorded: pg 212

BEAR, Michael - Franklin Twp., weak. Wife: Catharine; children: Henry, Andrew, Easter, Michael, Christian, John, Martin, Magdalena, Mary; executors: Henry HOOVER, Jacob SHENK (renounced); witnesses: David, John, Samuel REIF; written: 10 Oct 1808; probate: 15 Jul 1809; recorded: pg 57

WILL BOOK B

BEARD, John - Liberty Twp., farmer and cooper, sick. Wife: Mary; apprentice: Henry FERGUSON; executors: wife, James MAGINLY; witnesses: William MCCLELLAN, Isaac MOORE; written: 15 Dec 1809; probate: 26 Mar 1810; recorded: pg 72

BENDER, John - Menallen Twp., weak. Wife: Catharine; children: Jacob, John, Polly, Hanah, Elizabeth wife of John HEWITT, Catharine PLANK, Sarah MILLER, Mary, Eve, Julian, Margaret; executors: son John, George WIGON; witnesses: Conrad BENDER, Daniel RICE, William SLAYBAUGH; written: 29 May 1816; probate: 24 Jun 1816; recorded: pg 482

BERNINGER, Henry - Oxford town, Adams County, sick. Wife: Mary Ann; stepdaughter: Margaret; bequest to Roman Cath. Ch. at Conewago; executors: wife, Tobias KEPNER; witnesses: Henry HEAGEN, John SHEAFFER; written: 1 Jan 1813; probate: 21 Apr 1813; recorded: pg 224

BIGHAM, William - Liberty Twp., sick. Wife: mentioned; children: James, Thomas, Hugh, Charles (last three land in Butler Co., Pa.), John, Armor, Anna Eliza, William; executors: sons Hugh, James; witnesses: James CUNNINGHAM, John MCCONAUGHY; written: 27 Jan 1816; probate: 7 Feb 1816; recorded: pg 450

BITTINGER, Christina - Berwick Twp., widow, weak. Daughters: Christina, Margaret, Magdalena, Barbara, Elizabeth, Susanna, Mary; executors: son-in-law Tobias KEPNER, John NOLL; witnesses: Sebastian HEFER, George HENRY; written: 10 May 1806; probate: 9 Jun 1812; recorded: pg 195

BITTINGER, Michael - Franklin Twp., yeoman, sickly. Wife: Elizabeth; children: Jacob, Frederick, Elisabeth BALSLY, Michael, Susanah MINDER, Peggy FOAL(?), Andrew, Catharine COVER(?), Poley CROSS, Christiana HUSEL(?), Mary; executors: sons Jacob, Andrew; witnesses: Jacob BUSHEY, Jacob SANBLE; written: Mar 1811 (no day); probate: 20 Jun 1812; recorded: pg 198

BLACK, Ann - Mt Joy Twp., weak. Children: Rachel wife of Samuel LINN, Sarah wife of Aaron DEVENY; grandchildren: James LINN, Ann wife of Robert MCCREARY, Rachel wife of Philip HEAGY, John LINN, James BLACK; great grandchildren: Robert LINN of John, Robert BLACK of James, Ann DEVENY of Sarah; executors: grandson James BLACK, nephew John BLACK; witnesses: Edward HEGAN, John W. BLACK; written: 13 Apr 1808; probate: 10 May 1808; recorded: pg 13

BLACK, James - Mt Joy Twp. Nephews: Robert, James, John W. BLACK, Thomas W. BLACK son of brother Henry; bequests to: George HEAGY husband of Elizabeth BLACK, Ann MCCREARY wife of Robert, Sarah wife of Hugh DUNWOODY, James B. HEAGY, son of Philip, Rachel HEAGY wife of Philip; executors: nephews James and Thomas W. BLACK; witnesses: John MCKINNEY, John MCCONAUGHY; written: 18 Jun 1816; probate: 9 Jul 1816; recorded: pg 486

BLIVER, Adam - Berwick Twp., old and weak. Wife: Margaret; children: Christina, Adam, Susanna, Catherina (deceased), Elizabeth, Margaret; grandchildren: John HOFFMAN, Elizabeth wife of Adam ----; executors: Tobias KEPNER, Charles WILKESON (renounced); witnesses: Nicholas HENRY, Conrad FANERSTOCK; written: 17 Oct 1813; probate: 5 Apr 1815; recorded: pg 386

BOWER, Michael - Huntington Twp. Wife: Elizabeth; children: Catharine wife of John KEL--, residing in Berks Co., from first wife, Jacob, Daniel, Michael, David, Frederick, Samuel, Anna Maria, Margaret; executors: son David, Daniel SHEFFER Esq.; witnesses: John FICKES, Fletcher MOORHEAD; written: 9 Jul 1814; probate: 25 Dec 1815; recorded: pg 442

BRANDON, George - Huntington Twp., sick. Nephew: George Washing(ton) BRANDON; siblings: Elezer, Joshua, Ebenezer, Joseph, Miriam wife of William HALL, Lettice wife of Samuel CROSS, Mary wife of Robert NICKEL; brother-in-law, James BRANDON; executor: John SADLER; witnesses: Templeton BRANDON, George SMITH; written: 11 Nov 1814; probate: 8 Jan 1816; recorded: pg 445

WILL BOOK B

BRANDON, Thomas - Huntington Twp. Children: James, Templeton, Martha wife of George SMITH, Sarah wife of Robert MOORHEAD, Elizabeth wife of Archibald MCGREW, Thomas, Jane; grandchildren: James and Jane MCGREW, James of James, Thomas LONG son of Templeton, Thomas son of Martha, the last three grandsons to be taught to read Holy Scripture; executors: sons James and Templeton BRANDON, James ROBINETTE; witnesses: Eliezer BRANDON, Samuel WHITE; written: 25 Sep 1810; probate: 14 Nov 1810; recorded: pg 91

BRANNER, Michael - Adams County, weak. Wife: Ann; children: Maria CLARK, Michael, George, Elizabeth BUMGARDTNER, Frederick; executors: son-in-law Peter BUMGARTNER, Jacob WINEBRIGHT; witnesses: Jacob MUNDORFF, John MCMALEN, Daniel SCHOENER; written: 23 Jul 1800; codicil written: 1 Apr 1806 witnessed by William PATTERSON, Jacob MUNDORFF, Michael WAYBRIGHT; probate: 9 Dec 1807; recorded: pg 62

BRANON, William - Menallen Twp., yeoman, weak. Siblings: James, Agness BRITAN; aunts: Margaret and Hannah BLECKLEY; executors: uncle James BLECKLEY, Franklin Twp., aunt Hanah BLECKLEY, Menallen Twp.; witnesses: Peter STROSPER, Peter KECKLER; written: 17 May 1814; probate: 4 Jun 1814; recorded: pg 328

BRANWOOD, Sarah - Franklin Twp., widow, sick. Children: Sarah (a lunatic), Jane wife of James BLECKLEY Esq., Isabella; grandchildren: Sarah, Mary and Agness BLECKLEY, Mary JARDAN; executors: daughter Isabella, Alexander RUSSELL; witnesses: John HART, Alexander CALDWELL, James BLECKLEY; written: 1 Oct 1810; probate: 31 May 1814; recorded: pg 326

BRINKERHOF, George - Straban Twp., weak. Children: James, Rulip(?), Jacob, Gilbert, John, George; three old slaves Sam, Nick and Poll to be freed; executors: sons Gilbert, John and Henry; witnesses: John SHRIVER, David HERMAN; written: 22 Jun 1807; probate: 23 Jan 1810; recorded: pg 64

BROWN, Andrew - Hamiltonban Twp. Stepchildren: David and Margaret MCMULLEN; executors: stepson David, James GETTYS Esq; witnesses: William COBEAN, John MCCONAUGHY; written: 7 Feb 1814; probate: 18 Feb 1814; recorded: pg 288

BURKHOLDER, John - Latimore Twp., sick. Wife: Anna; children: Anna MUMPER, John, Catharine STROME, Henry, Elizabeth LATSHAW, Abraham, David, Samuel, Susanna KELLY, Mary, Rebeckah KITCH; executors: son Abraham, John BONNER; witnesses: Jacob KINERT, John ZEIGLER, Martin KITCH; written: 2 May 1808; probate: 21 Nov 1810; recorded: pg 97

BUSE, Peter - Germany Twp., weak, advanced in age. Children: Annamary, Elizabeth wife of Jonas MISSENHIMER, Dorothea wife of John MAHN, Christena wife of John HARRY(?), Peter (deceased), Catharine wife of Abraham JOHNS, Susana wife of John EYSTER, Eve (deceased)(her heirs), Barbara wife of George LONG; executor: son-in-law George LONG; witnesses: John WEIKART, Jacob SHEAFER; written: 9 Apr 1813; probate: 11 Jan 1816; recorded: 447

BUSHY, Nicholas - Reading Twp., old and weak. Wife: Margareth; children: mentioned with Peter (deceased) named; grandson: Jacob of Peter; executor: son Jacob; witnesses: Henry MYERS, Herman BLAESSER; written: 25 May 1808; probate: 19 Feb 1813; recorded: pg 220

CARBAUGH, Christian - Franklin Twp., weak. Wife: Susanna; children: Adam, Samuel, John, Martin, Christian, Catharine wife of Abraham SARAPH, Eve widow of Henry LANVER, Mary wife of Henry POTTORF, Christiana wife of John CARBAUGH, Elizabeth wife of Jacob WILKESON, Rachel wife of Henry SNYDER, Susanna (deceased) wife of George SNYDER; granddaughter: Eve SNYDER of Susanna; executors: sons Adam, Samuel; witnesses: Henry WERNER, Jacob BEESACKER, Peter MARK; written: 2 Oct 1813; probate: 27 Nov 1813; recorded: pg 276

WILL BOOK B

    CARLE, Michael - Berwick Twp., yeoman, old and weak. Wife: Susanna; children: Adam, Henry, Anna Mary wife of John SAELER, Susanna wife of Adam EICHELBERGER, George, Michael, David, Magdalen MATTER (last four deceased); grandchildren: Elizabeth and Catherine MATTER plus 7 other MATTER children; executors: son Adam, Jacob HOSTETTER; witnesses: Henry DANNER, Abraham KAGEY; written: 22 Feb 1811; codicil written: 8 Nov 1811; probate: 25 May 1813; recorded: pg 241
    CARRICK, John - Hamiltonban Twp. Children: John, Jane wife of David WAUGH, James, Moses, Nancy wife of James KERR, Samuel; grandchildren: John and Polly of John, William and John WAUGH, Polly WAUGH wife of Robert MCJENSEY(?), John and Polly of James, Montgomery of Moses, John and James KERR, Polly KERR wife of John COBEAN, John N. of Samuel; executors: William WAUGH Sr., David BLYTHE Sr.; witnesses: Alexander BRICE, Robert SLEMMENS Jr., Joseph MCGINLY; written: 9 May 1808; probate: 3 Mar 1812; recorded: pg 178
    CASSAT, Jacob - Adams County. Wife: Mary; children: Jacob, Kitty MAGAFFIN, Christine, Mary, Linah, Elizabeth, Margaret; bequest to Mary VANARSDAL; executors: Philip GRAFT, Jacob CASSAT Jr.; witnesses: James MAGAFFIN, Robert BELL; written: 17 Apr 1813; probate: 17 May 1813; recorded: pg 234
    CHAMBERLAIN, John - Reading Twp., unwell. Wife: Mary; son John, to be sent to college; Negro wench Nell to wife till aged 27, Negro wench Bets to be freed when aged 27, Negro boy Seb to be returned to brother James CHAMBERLAIN when Seb aged 21; executors: brother James, William WEAKLEY; witnesses: William HODGE, John B. ARNOLD, William PATTERSON; written: 22 Sep 1810; probate: 21 Nov 1810; recorded: pg 99
    CHAMBERLAIN, John - Franklin Twp., weak. Wife: Rebecca; children: Hannah, Rebecca; executors: John MCILNAY, Samuel WITHEROW; witnesses: John ROBISON, John MCILNAY, Samuel WITHEROW, John MICKLEY, Samuel KNOX; written: 7 Apr 1816; probate: 21 May 1816; recorded: pg 473
    CLUTS, Jacob - Adams County, weak. Wife: Barbara; children: Molly, Susannah, Rachel, George, Jacob, Joseph (all minors); executors: wife, brother John CLUTS; witnesses: Henry CLUTS, Michael ZEYER, John NULL; written: 3 Jan 1808; probate: 6 Aug 1808; recorded: pg 20
    COBEAN, Samuel - Franklin Twp. Children: Alexander, William, Samuel, John, James; Negro child Doll to William, Negro girl Feb to James, Negro woman Doll to be freed 1 Jan 1808, but any of her male children to James, females to Samuel; executors: sons Samuel, John; witnesses: Thomas WHITE, James G. PAXTON; written: 4 Apr 1804; probate: 31 Jan 1809; recorded: pg 33
    COLE, Elizabeth - Reading Twp., weak. Husband: Michael; children: Albertina wife of Anthony CRISSIMERE, George, Michael, Elizabeth wife of Jacob PHILIPS, Mary, Barbara wife of John LAMPIN, Molly wife of Mathias LAMPIN, Sarah, Christina, Catty, Jacob; executors: sons Michael, Jacob; witnesses: Simon PECHER, William PATTERSON; written: 14 Oct 1807; probate: 7 Dec 1807; recorded: pg 5
    COLTER, Elener - Straban Twp., weak. Siblings: John COLTER (his wife Sally), Josiah (his wife Agnes), Mary COLTER; niece: Susanah Kerr COLTER of Josiah; cousin: Giney KERR; tombstones for her and deceased sister Martha COLTER; executor: William KERR; witnesses: Armstrong and Margaret CAMPBELL; written: 12 Apr 1815; probate: 14 Aug 1815; recorded: pg 424
    CROSS, Thomas - Franklin Twp., weak. Wife: Elizabeth; children: William, Samuel, Martha MCMURRAY; grandchildren: John and Thomas of Samuel, son and daughter of William, sons and daughters of Martha; bequest to James DOBBIN Esq. and Martha VANEST(?); executors: Robert HAYES (renounced), James DOBBIN;

19

WILL BOOK B

witnesses: James YOUNG, John MARK; written: 25 Mar 1814; probate: 4 May 1814; recorded: pg 310
    CRUM, Francis - Menallen Twp., yeoman, very sick. Wife: Madlena; children: Levi, Moses, Casper, John, Peter, Henry, Barnhart, Solomon; executors: son John, Charles STEWART; witnesses: Nathan WRIGHT, Conrad BLANK, J. STEWART Jr.; written: 19 Jul 1813; probate: 16 Nov 1814; recorded: pg 357
    CULP, Christopher - Cumberland Twp. Wife: Catharine; children: Peter, Elizabeth wife of Adam HARTMAN, Christian, Matthias, Catharine, Mary wife of George STAULSMITH, Barbara wife of George CRESS, Susanna; executors: sons Christian, Matthias; witnesses: Horatio G. JAMESON, Francis STAULSMITH, Alexander RUSSELL; written: Dec 1805 (no day); probate: 21 Feb 1809; recorded: pg 37
    CUPSER, Christina - McSherrystown, widow, very weak. Bequest to children of Jacob KUPSER: Joseph, Molly wife of Peter HANDLEY, Barbara wife of Anthony FLESLEY, Elizabeth wife of John MOSER, Gitrille(?) wife of Henry ECK, Teresia wife of Conrad FINK; executors: Nicholas STORMBAUGH, John AULABAUGH; witnesses: Martin CLUNK, Daniel EYSTER; written: 26 Apr 1813; probate: 27 May 1813; recorded: pg 246
    DECKER, Frederick - Berwick Twp., very sick. Wife: Barbara; children: mentioned; executors: Samuel SMITH, Tobias KEPNER; witnesses: Nehemiah HOWEL, Catharine DEEL; written: 26 Sep 1816; probate: 11 Oct 1816; recorded: pg 496
    DEFFENDAL, Barbara - Mt Joy Twp., widow of John, weak. Children: John, Catharine HERTER, Barbara GROSS, Mary RIDDLEMOSER, Philip, (children of) Samuel, (children of) Margaret RIFFEL, Abraham; bequest to Catholic Church of Conewago; executors: son Abraham, Jacob RIDER; witnesses: R. MCILHENNY, Anthony ROSE, Jacob SHRIVER; written: 30 Nov 1805; probate: 4 Jun 1810; recorded: pg 79
    DEMAREE, David - Mt Pleasant Twp. Will signed DEMAREST. Wife: Leana; children: Cornelius, Luke, Albert, Charity wife of Hezekiah HOUGHTALING, Hannah wife of Thomas JONSTON, Katherine wife of Mathias VANTINE, Sarah 'who was wife of Daniel COMMONGORE, (all previous children identified as from 'last wife', David, Garrat; executors: wife, sons David, Cornelius; written: 1 Feb 1785; witnesses: George BRINKERHOFF, Daniel BROWN, David BEATY Jr.; codicil: 28 Nov 1801 mentions stepdaughter (from 'last wife') Elizabeth wife of Gilbert BRINKERHOFF, witnessed by George, Garret and John BRINKERHOFF; probate: 7 Jan 1809; recorded: pg 68
    DICKSON, Samuel - Straban Twp., weak. Siblings: Margaret BROWN, James; nieces and nephew: Maria, Wilamina and James of James; executors: Robert MCILHINEY, John KING; witnesses: Hugh and Abraham KING, Richard BROWN; written: 6 Jun 1809; probate: 12 Aug 1809; recorded: pg 59
    DIEHL, Frederick - Menallen Twp. Wife: Mary; children: Jacob, John, David, Abraham, Samuel, Mary, Hannah, Elizabeth; grandchildren: Elizabeth, Mary, Sally and Joseph of Abraham; executors: sons Jacob and John, son-in-law David PFOUTZ; written: Aug 1814, no day; codicil written 9 May 1816 witnessed by Jacob DELLONE, Herman BLAESSER; witnesses: Emanuel and George ZIEGLER, George WELSH; probate: 8 Jun 1816; recorded: pg 478
    DILL, Ester - Frederick County, now Germany Twp., Adams Co., widow of Nickles, weak and frail. Children: Nickles, Hannah widow of Jacob PARR; grandchildren: Eistie DILL now KUNS, Hanah DILL now BANKERD, Elizabeth DILL now MOUSE, Cetey DILL now BEHTEL, Elizabeth PARR now RIDER, Cetey PARR now GILESPY, Rachel PARR wife of Joseph RIDER, Hanah, Ester and Jacob PARR; bequest to friend Philip LONG/LONGSINER; executor: friend; witnesses: William KERR, Michael SNYDER, William LEIDNER; written: 10 Aug 1812; probate: 14 Jun 1813; recorded: pg 250

WILL BOOK B

DILL, Mathew - Millerstown, yeoman. Wife: Susana; children: George, Betsey wife of Thomas SANDERSON (land in Dills Branch, Indiana Co., Pa.), Jean/Tean wife of John CALHON (also land in Ind. Co.), John, Thomas, Mary WILLIAMS, Martha DISCON(?), Matthew, Nancy, Armor, Abagail RITCHEY; stepdaughter: Mary WAUGH; grandchildren: Matthew and George of George; executors: Amos MAGINLY Esq and Thomas MCKEE; written: 5 May 1811; witnesses: William and John PAXTON, David MCCLELLAN; codicil: 5 Jan 1812 witnessed by John PAXTON, Jacob HEAGY, David MCCLELLAN; probate: 30 Apr 1812; recorded: pg 186

DILL, Susannah - Hamiltonban Twp., weak. Children: Polly wife of John KERR (to have servant girl Rose), Susannah wife of Thomas MCKEE, Samuel WAUGH, Nancy wife of William KING, William WAUGH, James WAUGH; granddaughters: Susan Matilda WAUGH, Nancy MCKEE; executors: sons-in-law Thomas MCKEE, John KERR; witnesses: Joseph MCGINLEY, Zephaniah HERBERT, Ezra BLYTHE; written: 13 May 1815; probate: 30 Dec 1816; recorded: pg 509

DOBBIN, Alexander - Cumberland Twp., minister of the Gospel. Wife: Mary (to get remaining time of Negro Lett); children: Matthew, Alexander, James, Daniel, Mary, Isabella; executors: sons James, Matthew; witnesses: Joseph WORLEY, William G. MCPHERSON; written: 20 Dec 1808; probate: 7 Jun 1809; recorded: pg 50

DOTTERER, Conrad - Conewago Twp., weak, advanced in age. Children: Conrad, John, George, Elizabeth (deceased), Margaret (deceased), Michael, Annamaria wife of Jonathan ROUTSON, Juliana wife of Frederick SPONSELLER, Frederick; all children and children of Elizabeth and Margaret received land in 'Lisbon and Columbiana County (Ohio) in Mill Creek Settlement'; executors: sons John, George; witnesses: Philip RAHN, John WEIKERT; written: 26 Jan 1808; probate: 16 Feb 1808; recorded: pg 8

DUNWOODY, Jane - Hamiltonban Twp., weak. Children: Rosanna wife of James DOWNEY(?), Jane wife of Samuel FERGUSON, Sarah wife of James PATTON, Hugh, Isabella wife of James REID, Robert, Daniel (deceased); father: John CRAWFORD (deceased); husband: Hugh DUNWOODY (deceased); female slave Violet to be freed; executors: David BLYTHE, Joseph MCGINLEY; witnesses: Benjamin and John R. REID, Alexander RUSSELL; written: 27 Sep 1806; probate: 1 May 1811; recorded: pg 159

ECKENRODE, Henry Sr. - Berwick Twp., sick. Wife: Christina; six children including Catharine, Conrad; executor: wife; witnesses: John MARSHALL, Tobias KEPNER; written: 31 May 1806; probate: 28 Oct 1813; recorded: pg 272

EDIE, Samuel - Cumberland Twp. Children: John, Margaret wife of Robert STUART, James, David, Jennet wife of Samuel KYLE; executors: sons John, David; witnesses: George and Andrew BLANK, Thomas SWENEY; written: 12 Jan 1809; probate: 11 Mar 1809; recorded: pg 39

EIGHHOLTZ, George - Tyrone Twp., yeoman, sick. Wife: Elizabeth; sons: George, John; brother: Peter EIGHHOLTZ; executors: son George, Peter MILLER; witnesses: Jacob FITTER, Henry SCHMUSER; written: 17 Jan 1814; probate: 14 May 1814; recorded: pg 320

EKERT, John - Germany Twp., weak. Wife: Catharine; children: Peter, John, Abraham, Catharine BAKER; executors: sons John, Abraham; witnesses: Andrew and David SHRIVER, Michael MUSSEAR; written: 8 Dec 1810; probate: 22 Mar 1816; recorded: pg 464

ERVIN, Thomas - Hamilton Twp., weak. Wife: Sarah; children: mentioned; executor: wife; witnesses: John SOUN, Daniel SLAGLE; written: 16 Dec 1810; probate: 5 Feb 1811; recorded: pg 135

EWING, Samuel - Mt Pleasant Twp., old and infirm. Wife: Elizabeth; children: William, Catharine, Alexander, Robert; executors: son Robert, James

WILL BOOK B

HORNER; witnesses: Robert MCILHINNY, M. LOCKHART, Joseph KUHN; written: 19 Oct 1804; probate: 23 Mar 1809; recorded: pg 40
    FALEX, John - Berwick Twp., very sick. Children: John, Francis, Joseph, Mary wife of John LARENCE, Magdalena wife of Christian LARENCE, Catherine wife of Peter MARSHALL, Margaret, Nancy; executors: sons John, Francis; witnesses: Jacob ADAMS, Samuel LILLY, Nicholas NOEL; written: 11 Jan 1815; probate: 1 Feb 1815; recorded: pg 373
    FICKES, Valentine Sr. - Huntington Twp., weaver, weak. Wife: Barbara; children: Valentine, Benjamin, Rebeccah wife of Jacob FISKES Sr., Abraham, Daniel, John, Barbara, Jacob, Catherine, Mary, Susannah, Sarah; executors: son Abraham, brother John FICKES Esq.; witnesses: Abraham FICKES, James NEELY; written: 29 Jan 1815; probate: 16 Feb 1815; recorded: pg 377
    FICKLE, William - Latimore Twp., sick. Wife: Susannah; children: Margaret HOFFMAN, Juliana, Susannah, Sidny, Rachel, Joseph, Hannah, George Washington, Mary MYERS, Henry, John; grandchildren: Lidia and George MYERS; executors: John BONNER, Francis COULSON Esq.; witnesses: Andrew LOBAUGH, Michael RIPPERTON; written: 19 Apr 1813; probate: 3 Jun 1813; recorded: pg 248
    FEESER, Nicholas - Germany Twp., sick. Wife: Elizabeth; children: Catharine, Magdalen SHILT, others; executors: wife, sons-in-law Peter SHILT, George BAUM; witnesses: Robert MCILHINNY, Abraham KUNTZ; written: 4 Nov 1815; probate: 1 Dec 1815; recorded: pg 435
    FELTY, Diedrick - Berwick Twp., sick. Wife: Mary; children: John, Egnatius, Mary, Caty, Anna Joanna; executor: Caleb BRIEGNER; witnesses: Tobias KEPNER, William JENKINS; written: 20 May 1816; probate: 17 Jun 1816; recorded: pg 476
    FINK, Conrad - Berwick Twp., wagon maker, very sick. Wife: Teresia; three children; executors: brother Henry FINK, brother-in-law Joseph SNEERINGER; witnesses: Joseph MARSHALL, John AULABAUGH; written: 14 May 1815; probate: 5 Jun 1815; recorded: pg 413
    FISSEL, Philip - Tyrone Twp. Children: Henry, Catharine wife of Peter SCHLOSSER, Margaret, Elizabeth wife of John SOWERS; bequests to: Samuel and Margaret DICKSON, children of Mary FISSEL (deceased) wife of John DICKSON Jr.; executors: Henry SCHRIVER, John SOWERS; witnesses: Conrad SCHLOSSER, Jacob MILLER, Solomon HARRIS; written: 23 Aug 1816; probate: 31 Aug 1816; recorded: pg 493
    FLEAK, Catherine - Petersburg (York Springs), Huntington Twp., very sick. Son: Thomas CANAN; executor: Jacob GARDNER, renounced; son appointed admin; witnesses: John FICKES, William THOMPSON; written: 20 Dec 1810; probate: 8 Aug 1814; recorded: pg 349
    FLECK, Barbara - Franklin Twp., mariner, very sick. Children: Philip, Valentine, David, Jacob, Daniel, Nicholas, Elizabeth BOWER; son-in-law Henry ALGIST; grandchildren: William, Daniel, George, Valentine of Daniel, Samuel of Elizabeth, Barbara ALBERT; executors: sons Daniel, Nicholas; witnesses: Arthur NICKEL, James BLECKLY, Richard PROCTOR; written: 2 Jul 1808; probate: 23 Jul 1808; recorded: pg 18
    FLEMING, Sarah - Gettysburg, very sick. Brothers-in-law: John EWING, James COBEAN; aunt: Widow ELDER; nephews: Fleming and Andrew EWING; bequests to: Nancy MURPHY, Mrs. MCDERMAND and her daughter Catharine, Polly EWING, Jane ROWAN, children of sister Betsey wife of James COBEAN; land from estate of John FLEMING; niece: Sally Fleming COBEAN of Betsey; executor: John MCCONAUGHY; witnesses: Catharine MCPHERSON, William LINN, Alexander RUSSELL; written: 6 Apr 1815; probate: 8 Apr 1815; recorded: pg 398
    FLEMING, William - Straban Twp., yeoman, weak. Wife: Mary; children: John, George, others; executors: John KERR, William GILLELAND; witnesses:

WILL BOOK B

Nicholas DIETRICH, William GILLELAND Jr., John GOLDEN Jr.; written: 14 May 1816; probate: 19 Aug 1816; recorded: pg 490
    FLETCHER, Esther - Cumberland Twp., widow of Charles FLETCHER, sick. Children: Jennet, James, David; executors: sons James, David; witnesses: Archibald BOYD, Alexander RUSSELL; written: 4 Dec 1816; probate: 22 Jan 1817; recorded: pg 512
    FLETCHER, John - Franklin Twp., old and weak. Children: Thomas, Archibald, Mary wife of James GILCHRIST, Sarah wife of Samuel MCMULLEN, John (deceased); grandchildren: Archibald, John, Eve Esther wife of Edward FLETCHER, children of John; executors: grandson Archibald FLETCHER, Alexander RUSSELL; witnesses: Henry HOKE, James BROWN, J. MCCONAUGHY; written: 16 Feb 1808; codicil: 13 May 1809 now residing 'when at home' in Allegheny Co., Pa., witnessed by David MCCONAUGHY, James BROWN, James GILCHRIST; probate: 5 May 1812; recorded: pg 189
    FOALS, David - Menallen Twp. Children: Jacob, Elizabeth wife of Michael HOFMAN, Magdalena wife of Michael BILLINGER, Catharine wife of George STOUGH, John; executors: Thomas SELIX, Conrad PLANK; witnesses: Casper CRUM, John ARENDT; written: 12 Oct 1809; probate: 28 Dec 1812; recorded: pg 210
    FREED, Peter - Conewago Twp., farmer, sick. Wife: Magdalena; children: Jacob, Magdalena wife of John WISLER, Elizabeth wife of Adam LEONARD, Ester wife of Henry WISLER, Mary wife of H. WISLER, Catharina wife of Samuel BRILHART, Susanna FLORI (deceased), Nancy wife of Jacob GILBERT, Peter, Benjamin; grandchildren: Polly of Elizabeth, John of Susanna FLORI; executors: Jacob METZGER, John ERESMAN; witnesses: Christian FREED, John YOUNG, P. MILLER; written: 26 Jan 1808; probate: 1 Dec 1808; recorded: pg 26
    FREISE, George - Germany Twp. Wife: Mary Elizabeth; five children including Catharina JONSTON, Mary CERERSHTER(?), Betsey BARE, Simon; executors: son Simon, Philip LONGSINER; witnesses: William KERR, Jacob BROTHERS, Ludwig KOENIG; written: 15 Jun 1812; probate: 1 Feb 1815; recorded: pg 375
    GALBRAITH, John - Menallen Twp. Children: Mary wife of William GILLILAND, John, Jane, Margaret, Ann, Rosanna, William; grandchildren: Jane and Margaret of John; black man Tom to daughters; executors: sons John, William; witnesses: John MCGREW, William MCGREW Sr. and Jr.; written: 5 Dec 1811; probate: 21 Apr 1814; recorded: pg 307
    GALLAHER, Ellenor - Mt Pleasant Twp., very sick. Bequests to: Ellennor daughter of Daniel GALLAHER, niece Harriet of Edward GALLAHER, brother James GALLAHER, Rev. DEBARTH of Conewago Congregation, the Catholic nunnery at Emmitsburg; mother mentioned; executor: brother Edward; witnesses: John SNYDER, Annistateous GALLAHER, Jacob ADAMS; written: 7 Feb 1814; probate: 4 Mar 1814; recorded: pg 290
    GALLAHER, Judith - Mt Pleasant Twp., widow of Patrick GALLAHER, very weak. Children: Barnibas, James, Polly, Catherine, Christina, Em, Daniel; executor: Jacob ADAMS; witnesses: Jacob and George SLAGLE, Barney GALLAHER; written: 22 Mar 1814; probate: 21 Feb 1816; recorded: pg 459
    GARRETSON, John - Latimore Twp., weak. Wife: Mary; children: Hannah, Mary, Rachel, Isaac, John, Amos, Josiah, Joel, Susana PIDGEON, Constant RUSSELL; executors: sons John, Josiah, Joel, son-in-law Jesse RUSSELL; witnesses: John FICKES, Isaac PEARSON; written: 13 Dec 1810; probate: 22 Dec 1810; recorded: pg 102
    GETTYS, James - Gettysburg, weak. Wife: Mary; sons: James, Robert Todd; mulatto girl Sidney to wife; executors: wife, Alexander COBEAN Esq.; witnesses: James ROWAN, Mary PAXTON, Alexander RUSSELL; written: 11 Mar 1815; probate: 18 Mar 1815; recorded: pg 394

WILL BOOK B

GHESLER, Henry - Menallen Twp., weak. Wife: Susannah; children: Mary CONROD(?), Susannah GICE, Barbara HIMES, Magdalana CARSON; executors: John CARSON, Adam GICE; witnesses: Benjamin HARRIS, Samuel WRIGHT; written: 17 Feb 1809; probate: 7 Apr 1812; recorded: pg 181

GIBSON, William Sr. - Mt Joy Twp., weak. Wife: Anny; stepson: George CRIN; nephew: William GIBSON; executors: stepson and John REISE; witnesses: John WEIKERT, Henry ERBACH(?), John REEVER; written: 30 May 1811; probate: 16 Jul 1811; recorded: pg 165

GILLILAND, Samuel - Menallen Twp., weak. Children: John, Samuel, Ann, Sarah, Mary, Jean/Jane wife of Caleb HARLEN; executors: son John, brother William; witnesses: George MEICHL, John DULL, John EBERT; written: 26 Aug 1812; probate: 21 Oct 1812; recorded: pg 204

GOUDEY, Agness - Franklin Twp. Bequests to: George and David SCOTT of George SCOTT, Agness, Samuel and Jennet SCOTT of Richard SCOTT, Mary LEATHERWOOD, Sarah wife of John EARLY, William HAMILTON; executor: William HAMILTON; witnesses: David MCCLURE, John GROSS, Adam GMINDER; written: 5 Dec 1803; probate: 29 Jan 1808; recorded: pg 7

GRACELY, Michael - Straban Twp., sick. Wife: Mary; children: John, Lean, George, Mary (all minors); executors: wife, Christian THOMAS; witnesses: Samuel SMITH, John LEINERT; written: 15 Mar 1817; probate: 9 Apr 1817; recorded: pg 519

GRAHAM, Robert - Gettysburg. Wife: Margaret; nephews and niece: Samuel, Robert GRAHAM (of New York) and Widow LEECH of John GRAHAM (deceased), William son of William GRAHAM (deceased), Rev. Robert GRAHAM; executors: wife, Rev. Robert GRAHAM, Andrew MCILVAIN Esq.; witnesses: Thomas MCKELIP, Alexander RUSSELL, Alexander RUSSELL Jr.; written: 27 Apr 1813; probate: 20 May 1815; recorded: pg 411

GRIFFITH, Joseph - Menallen Twp., weak. Daughter: Ester wife of Christian BUSH; grandsons: John and Joseph BUSH; executors: John BUSH; witnesses: John BENDER, David MEALS, George WILSON; written: 12 Oct 1809; probate: 3 Nov 1809; recorded: pg 61

HALL, William - Cumberland Twp., weak. Daughter: Nancy wife of William FILLEN; grandchildren: Margret, Jane, Nancy and William of Nancy; nephews and niece: James, John, Samuel Hall, Alexander Ellis, William and Esther WILLIAMS; executors: William HAMILTON, John EDIE; witnesses: William MCCLEARY, James FLETCHER, Alexander RUSSELL; written: 7 Apr 1809; probate: 9 Apr 1810; recorded: pg 74

HAMMOND, Margaret - Tyrone Twp., weak. Mother: Mary HAMMOND; executor: Finly MCGREW; witnesses: John WRIGHT, Ruth HAMMOND, George WILSON; written: 5 Sep 1810; probate: 2 Oct 1810; recorded: pg 88

HARTMAN, Philip Sr. - Berwick Twp., yeoman, old and weak. Wife: Margareth; children: Catharina, Philip, Abraham; grandson: Jacob NAGLE; executors: son Philip, Herman BLAESSER; witnesses: Samuel DEARDORFF, George BECKER; written: 2 Jun 1808; probate: 26 Jun 1809; recorded: pg 55

HATTEN, Leonard - Huntington Twp. Wife: Margaret; bequests to: Margaret wife of Thomas COOPER, Mary wife of Samuel KENEDY, Margaret wife of Thomas STEPHENS, Mary PITTENDORF, Edward son of uncle Lewis HATTEN, Edward, James, Jane BLACKBURN, Rachael MORISON(?) children of brother Robert HATTEN; executors: Edward HATTEN, Thomas STEPHENS; witnesses: Thomas PEARSON, James KENNEDY, Mary WICKET; written: 27 Dec 1811; probate: 2 Dec 1815; recorded: PG 431

HAYES, Patrick - Gettysburg. Children: Nancy (to receive Negro Deb), Robert; executors: son Robert, John MCCONAUGHY; witnesses: Alexander COBEAN, Walter SMITH; written: 18 Mar 1808; probate: 19 May 1809; recorded: pg 49

24

WILL BOOK B

HEIKES, Jacob - Latimore Twp., weak. Wife: Polly, abandoned him many years before and living with another man; children: David and Betsey (minors); executor: William PATTERSON; witnesses: Philip MYERS, Henry HIGAS; written: 10 Mar 1814; probate: 10 May 1814; recorded: pg 318

HERSHEY, Andrew - Huntington Twp. Children: Margret wife of Ludwick NULL, Jacob, Joseph, Andrew, Catharine wife of William COULOGUE, Benjamin, George, Samuel, John, Mary, Rebecckah; executors: Henry HOKE, Peter FENCE; witnesses: John MCGREW, Burkhart WERNER; written: 22 Jan 1810; probate: 13 Apr 1810; recorded: pg 73

HILL, William - Liberty Twp., yeoman, weak. Children: Joseph, Susanna, Mary, Robert, William, John, Martin, Samuel, James, Cathrine WALKER, Jean HART, Margaret wife of James MCCLEARY, Elizabeth wife of James DOUGLASS, Thomas, William; executors: sons Martin, Samuel; witnesses: Ezra BLYTHE, David MCCLELLAN, A. MCGINLY; written: 15 Jan 1812; probate: 17 Aug 1813; recorded: pg 255

HILLEBUSH, Bernhard - Conewago Twp., yeoman, very sick. Wife: Catherine; children: William, Jacob, Catharina; executors: wife, George STINE; witnesses: Joseph KITCHTON, John AULEBAUGH; written: 19 Mar 1814; probate: 14 Apr 1814; recorded: pg 303

HOFFMAN, Catharine - Mt Pleasant Twp., very sick. Children: John, Elizabeth wife of Henry CHAMBERS, Polly wife of Ignatius ADAMS, Marian wife of Stophel STORM; executors: John SHRIVER, Philip STAUB; witnesses: William KLINE, John CONRAD, John SHRIVER; written: 26 Dec 1810; probate: 26 Jan 1811; recorded: pg 133

HOFFMAN, Christina - Gettysburg, weak. Everything to executor: Nicholas CRONBAUGH; witnesses: John H. BEGEN, Henry HOKE; written: 23 Oct 1814; probate: 9 Nov 1814; recorded: pg 353

HOLLINGER, Christian - Hamilton Twp. Wife: Catherina; children: David, Jacob, Christopher, Samuel, John, Catharina; servant: Catherina DRAK(?); executors: Jacob and Samuel FAHNESTOCK; witnesses: Solomon WHISTLER, John BROWN, George FRAUSS(?); written: 19 Jun 1813; codicil: 23 Aug 1813; probate: 9 May 1814; recorded: pg 314

HOLLINGER, John - Hamilton Twp. Wife: Catherine; children: Polly, Jacob; brother Jacob to be guardian of children; executor: uncle Valentine HOLLINGER; witnesses: Jacob LOUR/SOUR, Samuel FAHNESTOCK; written: 28 Apr 1814; probate: 20 Sep 1814; recorded: pg 335

HOLLOBAUGH, Christopher - Mt Pleasant Twp. Wife: Cathrina; children: Mary wife of Michael GIMBER, Christopher, Martin, Susanna wife of Henry LITTLE, William (deceased), Cathrina (deceased) wife of Jacob ENK, Philip; William and Cathrina each had two children; executor: John SLAGLE; witnesses: Lindsey STURGEON, Mathias MARTIN; written: 21 Sep 1807; probate: 30 Sep 1812; recorded: pg 202

HORNBERGER, John - Mt Pleasant Twp., yeoman, weak. Wife: Christina; sons: John, Abraham (minors); executors: Conrad SNYDER, William FERGUSON; witnesses: Abraham TAWNEY, John BEEHER; written: 5 Jul 1812; probate: 13 Aug 1812; recorded: pg 200

JENKINS, Walter - Franklin Twp., sick. Nephew: Moses Jenkins of brother Moses (deceased); niece: Ann COULTER; granddaughters: Ann, Mary CROOKS; William MCPHERSON named guardian of nephew, granddaughters; executors: William MCPHERSON, William HAMILTON; witnesses: William MEREDITH, Francis MCNUTT, Alexander RUSSELL; written: 1 May 1814; probate: 6 May 1814; recorded: pg 312

KEARNEY, James - Carroll's Tract. Children: Judeth NOLAN, Mary NOLAN, Patrick, James, John, Nicholas, Marten, Elinor, Mary Ann; executors: son and daughters, Nicholas, Elinor, Mary Ann; witnesses: Joseph HUGHS, Patrick LORRE,

WILL BOOK B

Bartholomew MCCAFFREY; written: 26 Dec 1815; probate: 10 Jun 1817; recorded: pg 511
    KEAS, Elizabeth - Gettysburg, widow, weak. Children: Catharine wife of William HAMILTON, Margaret, Mary; grandson: James Stewart HAMILTON; executors: daughters Margaret and Mary; witnesses: William BUCHANAN, William GILLILAND; written: 8 Jun 1808; probate: 25 Aug 1813; recorded: pg 258
    KEAS, Margaret - Gettysburg, weak. Sisters: Catharine HAMILTON, Mary wife of William LOWREY; nieces and nephews: Mary HAMILTON now WILSON, Margaret Hannah Keas HAMILTON, John, James, William, Robert Long HAMILTON, John Keas LOWREY; deceased mother: Elisabeth KEAS; William GILLILAND Sr. appointed guardian of John K. LOWREY; executor: William GILLILAND Sr.; witnesses: William GARVIN, Thomas MCKALEB; written: 19 Jun 1816; probate: 13 Dec 1816; recorded: pg 507
    KELLENBERGER, Adam - Germany Twp., weak. Wife: Margaret; children: John, Mary; executors: wife, John L. HINKLE; witnesses: Robert JONES, Michael KITZMILLER; written: 16 Mar 1815; probate: 12 Apr 1815; recorded: pg 404
    KERR, George - Hamiltonban Twp. Wife: Mary; children: John, Martha wife of Samuel MCCULLOUGH, Mary wife of William FLEMING, Isabella wife of Isiah WHITE, Elizabeth wife of Hugh SCOTT; grandsons: George Kerr SCOTT, John Joseph KERR; Negro wench Mash and Negro boy Penn to wife; mulatto girl Feb to be freed when she was 21; Negro boy Jim to son John; executor: son John; witnesses: John IRVIN, John MCCONAUGHY; written: 18 Dec 1813; codicil: 9 Nov 1814 witnessed by Walter SMITH, John MCCONAUGHY; probate: 15 Feb 1815; recorded: pg 381
    KERR, Mary - Hamiltonban Twp., weak. Children: John, Martha wife of Samuel MCCULLOUGH, Mary wife of William FLEMING, Isabella wife of Isiah WHITE, Elizabeth wife of Hugh SCOTT; grandson: George Kerr SCOTT; Negro woman Mash to be freed; executor: son John; witnesses: James G. PAXTON, William MAXWELL, Joseph MCGAUGHY; written: 24 Apr 1815; probate: 4 Dec 1814; recorded: pg 433
    KING, Abraham Sr. - Germany Twp., weak. Wife: Margaret; sister: Marillis wife of Stephen WYBLE; bequest to children of brother George KING; bequest to children of "my former wife's two daughters" Catherine WERNER, Mary LIGHTNER; bequest to Joseph and Mary, children of George LIGHTNER with money to be held by Frederick BLACK; executors: Peter KRAPS Sr., Jacob BROTHERS; witnesses: Robert MCILHENNY, Jacob WINROTT, John ARNOLD; written: 3 Sep 1807; probate: 25 May 1813; recorded: pg 237
    KING, George - Germany Twp., sick. Wife: Fronica; children, mentioned; executors: Henry MILLER of Frederick Co., Md., Adam WINTRODE; witnesses: Robert MCILHENNY, Philip LONG, Jacob SELL; written: 20 Feb 1810; probate: 13 May 1816; recorded: pg 471
    KING, Hugh - Tyrone Twp., weak. Children: Martha, Abraham, Victor, Hugh, William, George Washington, Hervey, Jacob; granddaughters: Harriet, Abigail; anaaut0r0: Robert MCILHINEY, Abraham and John KING; witnesses: John DICKSON, John MAGOFFIN, Richard BROWN; written: 9 Mar 1810; probate: 24 May 1811; recorded: pg 163
    KING, Victor W. - Straban Twp. Wife: Jane; son: John (minor); sister: Agnes KING; executors: Hugh KING Sr., John DICKSON; witnesses: William SCOTT, John KING, James DICKSON; written: 20 Mar 1809; probate: 25 Mar 1809; recorded: pg 42
    KING, William - Straban Twp., blacksmith, sick. Wife: Ann; children: James, Hugh, Robert, John, Samuel, William, Ann wife of John LEVINGSTON, Vilet, Nancy; executors: sons John, Robert, James; witnesses: William SCOTT, John DARNELL, James ROWAN; written: 17 Feb 1815; probate: 27 Feb 1815; recorded: pg 392

26

WILL BOOK B

KITZMILLER, Jacob Sr. - Germany Twp. Wife: Elizabeth; seven children, names Martin; executors: sons-in-law George MOUSE, Henry KOHLSTOCK; witnesses: Robert MCILHINNY, Frederick KEEFER, David WILL; written: 29 Oct 1804; probate: 21 Oct 1808; recorded: pg 23
 KNOUFF, Adam - Germany Twp., weak. Wife and children mentioned, only John named; executor: Jacob WINTRODE Esq.; witnesses: Robert MCILHENNY, George and Henry KEEFER; written: 9 Jul 1810; probate: 19 Nov 1810; recorded: pg 95
 KNOUFF, John - Germany Twp., weak. Children: John, Elizabeth LOHR, Adam, Ann Mary, Margaret HASPELHORN, Anthony; executors: son Adam, John WEIKART; witnesses: Robert MCILHENNEY, Jacob LITTLE, Abraham KUNTZ; written: 12 Apr 1803; probate: 15 Dec 1808; recorded: pg 28
 KNOX, Samuel - Hamiltonban Twp., weak. Wife: Mary; children: Samuel, Margaret wife of Thomas COCHRAN Esq.; grandchildren: Eleanor and Samuel COCHRAN, John and Samuel KNOX; bequest to Negro servant Fawn; executors: son Samuel, son-in-law Thomas COCHRAN; witnesses: James DOUGLASS, Samuel and Walter SMITH; written: 28 Oct 1803; probate: 3 Dec 1808; recorded: pg 30
 KOCH, Joseph - Germany Twp., mason, very sick. Wife: Barbara; children: Maryan, John (crippled in one hand), Francis, Barbara, Joseph; executors: wife, Balser HILBERT; witnesses: Adam KELLENBERGER, Philip BARDT, Jacob ADAMS; written: 2 May 1811; probate: 23 May 1811; recorded: pg 162
 KRAFT, John - Conewago Twp., very sick. Bequest to Roman Catholic Church in Conewago; brother: Peter; brother-in-law: Sebastian WEBER; father: Michael; pastor: Rev. DEBARTH; executors: Joseph SNEERINGER, Samuel LILLY; witnesses: Jacob WEBER, J. L. GUBERNATOR; written: 13 May 1812; probate: 30 May 1812; recorded: pg 193
 KUHN, Catharine - Mt Pleasant Twp., widow of John. Bequest to Roman Catholic Church at Conewago; children: Eve FOLLER, Teresa MYERS, Henry, Margaret BREIGHNER, Jacob, Joseph, George, Christian; granddaughter: Catharine BREIGHNER; executors: son Jacob, son-in-law John FOLLER; witnesses: robert MCILHINNY, Jacob WINROTT; written: 20 Apr 1815; probate: 5 Jun 1815; recorded: pg 417
 LEAS, Leonard - Reading Twp., sick. Children: John, Leonard, Moses, David, Stephen, Joseph, George, Rebecah, Philip (deceased); grandson: Enos of Philip; Valentine HOLLINGER guardian of George and Rebecah; son Leonard guardian of Joseph; executors: son Leonard, Valentine HOLLINGER; witnesses: Moses LEAS, George BROWN; written: 4 Feb 1810; probate: 27 Feb 1810; recorded: pg 65
 LEHMAN, Christian - Menallen Twp., yeoman, very sick. Wife: Hannah; children: John, Christian, Mary, Rachel; executors: brother-in-law Jacob DEHL, John STEWART; witnesses: Michael MINIGH, John CLINE, Thomas COCHRAN; written: 2 Apr 1812; probate: 21 Apr 1812; recorded: pg 182
 LITTLE, Henry - Germany Twp., weak. Five sons, five daughters, only Jacob, Henry, David and Mary (deceased) named; Mary had 4 children; executors: Philip LONG, Jacob BROTHERS Sr.; will signed KLEIN; witnesses: Robert MCILHENNY, Daniel LONG, Jacob BOYER; written: 7 Mar 1810; probate: 7 Jan 1811; LONG renounced 26 Dec 1810, witnessed by John WEIKART, Jacob SELL; recorded: pg 105
 LOCKHART, Moses - Mt Pleasant Twp., weak. Wife: Margret; children: Polly, James, Moses, Samuel, Ephraim; executors: son Moses, William HODGE; witnesses: Ludwick WAGGONER, Alexander and Robert EWING; written: 27 May 1810; probate: 2 Jun 1810; recorded: pg 77
 LOHR, Margaret - Germany Twp. Children: Abraham, Jacob, Andrew, John (deceased), Adam, Martin, Catharine wife of Philip SHALL, Christina wife of Samuel GOBRICHT; grandson: Martin of John; executors: son Martin, Frederick

WILL BOOK B

BENTZ; witnesses: George NACE, John SHALL; written: 5 Oct 1813; probate: 2 Jul 1816; recorded: pg 485

LONG, Peter - Hamilton Twp., farmer, very sick. Wife: Christina; children: Adam, George, Catharine, Mary, Elizabeth, Peter, John, Margaret, Christina, Luis; Catharine and Mary married; bequest to Parson MARSHALL at Roman Catholic Church at Conewago; executors: son Adam, Tobias KEPNER; witnesses: Henry GITT, Henry MYERS; written: 2 Mar 1817; probate: 11 Apr 1817; recorded: pg 520

LORRIMER, Thomas - Mt Joy Twp. Wife: Catharine; children: William, Thomas, Margaret wife of James DUFF, Mary wife of Moses MCELWAIN, Sidney wife of William JOHNSTON, Nancy wife of John JOHNSTON, Elizabeth wife of Robert BOYD; executors: son-in-law Moses MCELWAIN, George SHEKLY; witnesses: Moses JINKINS, William SHEKLY, Alexander RUSSELL; written: 9 Dec 1809; probate: 9 Sep 1816; recorded: pg 494

MAXWELL, William - Gettysburg, attorney, counselor at law. Wife: Sophia, to receive yellow girl Molly; sons: Robert Smith, William, George Lashells, Ralph; guardians for sons: Ralph LASHELLS, Robert HAYES; executors: Alexander COBEAN, Samuel HUTCHISON, merchants of Gettysburg; witnesses: James DOBBIN, Walter SMITH; written: 7 Feb 1816; probate: 12 Feb 1816; recorded: pg 453

MCALLEN, Thomas - Cumberland Twp. Wife: Elizabeth, now pregnant; second daughter: Jane; uncle: Thomas, late of Londonderry Twp., Dauphin Co., Pa.; executors: John STEWART, John SPEER; witnesses: William MCCURDY, William COCHRAN, John MORROW; written: 1 Jun 1808; probate: 9 Jun 1808; recorded: pg 14

MCCLELLAN, Mary - Cumberland Twp., widow of William, weak. Sons: Samuel, David; bequest to Kitty DEVER; executors: son Samuel, David WILSON; witnesses: David EDIE, John HARSHEY; written: 1 Jul 1808; probate: 3 Aug 1808; recorded: pg 19

MCCONAUGHY, David - Menallen Twp., weak. Children: Margaret, Martha wife of David EDIE, David, Sarah wife of John EDIE, Robert (deceased), Elizabeth wife of Robert MORISON(?), Ann wife of William EWING, Jane widow of Thomas EWING; five children of Robert; Negro Phillis to Margaret; Negro Abby to be supported by the estate; executors: John EDIE, John MCCONAUGHY; witnesses: William HAMILTON, George and William SHEKLEY; written: 9 May 1809; probate: 21 Dec 1815; recorded: pg 440

MCCURDY, Robert - Cumberland Twp., sick. Children: William, Robert, Nancy PAXTON, James, Margret wife of George SHEKELY, Martha wife of Samuel TAGGART, Mary wife of Robert THOMPSON; grandson: Robert McCurdy PAXTON; executors: sons William, Robert; witnesses: Robert HAYES, David HORNER, Robert MAJOR; written: 5 Aug 1805; probate: 25 May 1810; recorded: pg 76

MCGREW, Alexander - Tyrone Twp. Children: William, Archibald, Jean wife of Solomon HANES, youngest daughter Mary wife of John DAVIS; grandchildren of Archibald; sister: Catharine COOPER, widow; bequest to Martha MCGREW wife of William BEALS; executors: son William, friends John and Finley MCGREW; witnesses: Martha, Mary and Nathan MCGREW; written: 1807 (no date); probate: 5 Jul 1808; recorded: pg 22

MCGREW, Martha - Huntington Twp., widow of Archibald. Sons: Alexander, John, Archibald, William (deceased); grandchildren: Archibald and Mary of Alexander, Martha and Mary of John, Martha CARSON wife of ORR(?) and Boondon(?,female), John and Hester FLETCHER, Catherine BOYD, Archibald and Mary of Archibald, William W. and Maria of William; great grandson: James of Archibald of John; executor: son John; witnesses: Nathan and Finley MCGREW; written: 19 Jun 1807; probate: 9 May 1812; recorded: pg 191

WILL BOOK B

MCGREW, William - Menallen Twp. Wife: Mary, bound girl Maria KOTT to wife; children: William, John, James, Elizabeth, Alexander, Robert; executors: sons William, James; witnesses: David STEWART, Frederick and George EICHOLTZ; written: 16 May 1814; probate: 15 Nov 1814; recorded: pg 355

MCILVAIN, Andrew - Mt Pleasant Twp. Wife: Mary; children: Robert, William, ALexander, Moses, Andrew, John, Mary wife of Richard KNIGHT, Rebeccah, Margaret; grandchildren: Jesse, Ann, Rebeccah and newborn daughter KNIGHT; executors: sons Robert, William; witnesses: James HORNER, John SNYDER, Alexander RUSSELL; written: 9 May 1807; probate: 12 Mar 1811; recorded: pg 145

MCKNIGHT, James - Tyrone Twp., yeoman. Wife: Jane; children: William, Joseph, Francis, Sarah wife of John GALBREATH, Catharine, James, John; executors: sons James, John; witnesses: Finley and William MCGREW, John DUFFIELD; written: 11 May 1804; probate: 18 Feb 1811; recorded: pg 139

MCLAUGHLIN, Francis - Franklin Twp., weak. Parents: Francis and Briget, living in Kingdom of Great Britain; brother: John; executors: brother John, Peter MARKS (renounced); witnesses: Michael CRILLY, David NEWMAN; written: 3 Aug 1814; probate: 11 Aug 1814; recorded: pg 332

MCMORDIE, Jennet - Franklin Twp., weak. Children: Francis, Robert, Adam, John, Agness wife of Rev. William SPEAR, Jean Boyd ARMSTRONG; grandchildren: Robert and Jennet of Francis, Robert and Francis ARMSTRONG, Robert of Robert; executors: sons John, Robert; witnesses: John EDIE, Samuel WILSON (of Wash. Co., Pa. at probate); written: 30 Sep 1806; probate: 27 Jan 1809; recorded: pg 45

MCPHERSON, Robert - Cumberland Twp., very sick. Wife: Hannah; father: William; brother: John; land in Frederick Co., Md.; children: William, David and Robert Alexander; executors: father and brother; witnesses: David ERB, Reynolds MCPHERSON, Alexander RUSSELL; written: 3 Apr 1813; probate: 1 May 1813; recorded: pg 229

MCSHERRY, Catherine - Germany Twp., widow of Patrick, weak. Children: Catherine COALE, Sarah CLEMENTS, James; executor: son James; witnesses: Robert MCILHINNY, Jacob WILL Jr., Andrew WILL; written: 3 Jun 1802; probate: 25 May 1815; recorded: pg 239

MCVEAR, Alexander - Hamiltonban Twp. Wife: Margaret; children: Samuel, Isabella wife of James STEVENSON (of Kentucky), Agness, Margaret "lately intermarried with Thomas BIGHAM"; grandchildren: Alexander and Margaret STEVENSON; executors: wife and son; witnesses: John MCELNAY, Henry HOKE, Alexander RUSSELL; written: 13 Apr 1799; probate: 14 Oct 1816; recorded: pg 498

MILEY, John - Reading Twp., weak. Wife: Ann; children: Jacob, John (land in Westmoreland Co.), Abraham, Catharine wife of Jacob ?NOBARGER, Freany (deceased) wife of David KIMMEL, Ann wife of Adam MILLER; grandson: Samuel KIMMEL; executors: sons Jacob, John; witnesses: John HILDEBRAND, Jacob BRUCH, Samuel FAHNESTOCK; written: 20 Nov 1806; probate: 25 Sep 1810; recorded: pg 86

MILLER, Paul - Mt Pleasant Twp., advanced in age. Wife: Elizabeth; children: Lewis, John, Ignatius, Teresia wife of Nicholas NOEL, Magdalen wife of Adam SHORB, Paul; bequest to Rev. Lewis DEBARTH, Conewago Chapel; executors: son Ignatius, John AULABAUGH; witnesses: Philip and Andrew KOHLER; written: 28 Aug 1814; probate: 21 Sep 1815; recorded: pg 426

MONSHOUR, Nicholas - Germany Twp., weak. Wife: Margaret; children: John, Nicholas, Jacob, Henry, Catherine MARTIN, Hannah KOONS, Elizabeth GOOD, Sarah ECKART (deceased); grandchildren: John, David, Nancy, Esther and Sarah ECKART; executors: Samuel BECHER, David HOOVER; witnesses: Henry and Jacob KOONS, William KELLY; written: 20 Aug 1812; probate: 11 Oct 1813; recorded: pg 264

WILL BOOK B

MORROW, John - Hamiltonban Twp., frail. Children: Jeremiah, Margaret wife of Hugh DUNWOODY/DINWODY, Sarah, John, Mary, Rebecca, James, Jane, Martha; executors: son John (renounced), son-in-law Hugh DUNWOODY, Dr. Samuel KNOX; witnesses: David MOORE, James THOMPSON, Robert SPEAR; written: 6 Dec 1797; probate: 8 Aug 1811; recorded: pg 168

MORTON, John Sr. - Menallen Twp., weak. Wife: mentioned; children: Jesse, John, Mary wife of John BLACKBURN, Margret wife of William NEWLAND, Sarah wife of Archibald FLEMEN, Elizabeth wife of Isaac FISHER, Deborah wife of George HEWITT; executors: son Jesse, son-in-law George HEWITT; witnesses: Nathan HENDRICKS, John and William DELAP; written: 23 May 1795; probate: 22 Aug 1810; recorded: pg 83

MYER, Barbra - Adams Co., weak. Children: Cathrine ELDENDICE, Mary, John, Jacob, Martin, Daniel; executors: sons John, Jacob; witnesses: William BIGHAM, Nicholas MORITZ, Samuel WIAN (?); written: 29th, 1815; probate: 23 Nov 1815; recorded: pg 429

MYERS, Mary - town of Berlin, weak. Daughter: Peggy BENDER; grandchildren: Nancy and David JAMESON; executors: Frederick ASPER, Jacob MYERS; witnesses: John ATTIG, William PATTERSON; written: 26 Mar 1811; probate: 17 Apr 1811; recorded: pg 153

MYERS, Nicholas - Reading Twp., weak. Children: Nicholas, Sarah (deceased) wife of John GETS, Elizabeth widow of Anthony SWARTSMAN, Barbara wife of Jacob SHORP; grandsons: Jacob, John and William GETS of Sarah, seven by Elizabeth; executors: John HILDEBRAND, David MYERS; witnesses: Philip GELWICKS, John MILEY; written: 12 Apr 1805; probate: 8 Feb 1809; recorded: pg 35

NAGLE, John Sr. - town of Berlin, weak. Wife: Elizabeth; children mentioned; executor: son John; witnesses: Thomas REED, Henry FORREY, Samuel FAHNESTOCK; written: 15 Jan 1812; probate: 18 Jan 1813; recorded: pg 214

NICKEL, John - Tyrone Twp., weak. Wife: Elizabeth; he was executor of estate of James NICKEL Sr.; children: Robert, William, John, Sarah, Elizabeth; executors: John LEECE, Jonathan BOWER; witnesses: Nicholas and Ludwick GROOP; written: 15 Aug 1807; probate: 2 Dec 1807; recorded: pg 3

NOEL, Andrew - Menallen Twp., weak. Wife: Theresa; children: Jacob, Madalena wife of Thomas NOEL, Margaret wife of George STARNER, John, Susanna wife of Isaac WARREN, Nicholas, Catharine wife of John LOWSTETTER, Barbara wife of Frederick WARREN, Betsey wife of Paul MILLER, Theresa wife of David WARREN; executors: son-in-law Isaac WARREN, Alexander RUSSELL; witnesses: Abraham STRASBAUGH, John DILLON; written: 31 Oct 1816; probate: 11 Mar 1817; recorded: pg 516

NOLL, John - town of Berwick, house carpenter, very sick. Wife: Elizabeth; executors: brother-in-law Jacob WOLF, Jacob FAHNESTOCK; witnesses: Frederick BAUGHER, Tobias KEPNER; written: 30 Jul 1811; probate: 18 Oct 1812; recorded: pg 171

O'BLENIS, Peter - Berwick Twp. Mother: Mary; siblings: Sarah NEELY, Daniel, John, Elizabeth BATEMAN, Mary, Barbara, executors; sister Barbara, John CHAMBERLAIN; witnesses: Simon PECHER, David DEMARER, T. BAILY; written: 1 May 1808; probate: 27 Jun 1808; recorded: pg 16

OWINGS, Robert - McSherrystown, advanced in age. Daughter-in-law Theresia OWINGS, widow of Moisius(?) OWINGS; grandsons: Joseph Augustus and Eusebius Jacobus of Moisius; bequest to Roman Catholic Church at Conewago and the poor of the congregation; land in Cambria Co., Pa.; bequest to Rev. Augustin GALICIEN of the Roman Church Church at Loreto, Cambria Co. and to the poor of that congregation; executors: daughter-in-law and John AULEBAUGH;

WILL BOOK B

witnesses: John KUHN, J. L. GUBERNATOR; written: 12 Aug 1812; probate: 5 Dec 1814; recorded: pg 364

PATTERSON, Susanna - Hamilton Twp., weak. Children: Martha wife of Jacob GROSCOST, Susanna wife of Daniel GROSCOST, Margrate wife of Huey DIVIN, John, Samuel, Elisabeth wife of Jacob LINGEFELTER, Mary wife of Jacob KENEY, Isaac, James, Sholas; grandchildren: Sholases SHUSEY, Samuel SUSEY(?); executors: sons Samuel, James, Sholas; witnesses: Daniel and Elizabeth SLAGLE; written: 21 Mar 1811; probate: 12 Mar 1814; recorded: pg 291

PEARSEN, Thomas - Huntington Twp., weak. Wife: Martha; children: Hannah, Elias, Amelia, Phebe, Ann, Jodus(?), Lydia, Eliza, Thomas; executors: John MCGREN, brother Isaac PEARSEN, brother-in-law John EVERITT; witnesses: Richard PILKINGTON, Nicholas WIREMAN; written: 3 Apr 1814; probate: 19 Apr 1814; recorded: pg 305

PETTIT, Thomas - Latimore Twp., weak. Wife: Ann; children: John, Polly wife of George SHEFFER, Ann; bequest to David GILL; executors: son John, son-in-law George SHEFFER; witnesses: Andrew WOLF, Abraham LOBACHE; written: 3 Feb 1815; probate: 22 Feb 1815; recorded: pg 385

PFOUTZ, Michael - Cumberland Twp., sick. Wife: Susannah; only child: Catharine; executors: brother Peter, friend Michael BOSSERMAN; witnesses: Jacob PFOUTZ, Horatio G. JAMESON, Alexander RUSSELL; written: 28 Apr 1809; probate: 4 May 1809; recorded: pg 47

PILKINGTON, Vincent - Huntington Twp. Wife: Rebecka; sons: Thomas, Richard; executors: sons; witnesses: James and Allen ROBINETTE; written: 3 Nov 1810; probate: 12 May 1813; recorded: pg 230

PORTER, Thomas - Tyrone Twp., weak. Wife: Sarah; children: Joseph, David, Mary, Letitia, Thomas, Ann, Grizzy widow of Robert PORTER; grandchildren: Jane, Ann, James and Sarah of Grizzy; executors: sons Joseph, David; witnesses: Samuel NEELY Jr., James NEELY; written: 26 Sep 1804; probate: 11 Jan 1814; recorded: pg 281

PRESSELL, Michael Sr. - town of Berlin, old and weak. Children: Susanna, Mary wife of John BOWMAN, Elizabeth wife of George BAKER, Sabina wife of George MILHIME, Michael; executors: Isaac LATSHAW, Samuel FAHNESTOCK; witnesses: Dr. Daniel BAKER, Abraham MUMMERT; written: 17 Nov 1813; probate: 3 Oct 1814; recorded: pg 346

RANDOLPH, Nathaniel - Liberty Twp., sick. Wife: Agness; children: Ann, Rachel, Sarah, Maria, Nathaniel, Joseph, wife pregnant; bequest to daughter-in-law Ann widow of son Sell; executors: son Nathaniel, James MCCLEARY; witnesses: Job RANDOLPH, John BINGHAM, Alexander RUSSELL; written: 18 Jun 1816; probate: 15 Aug 1816; recorded: pg 488

RIDDLEMOSER, Michael Sr. - Germany Twp., weak. Wife: Elizabeth; children: mentioned but only Joseph named; executor: son Michael; witnesses: Robert MCILHENNY, Nicholas MONSHOWER, Ludwick SELL; written: 12 Aug 1808; probate: 14 Jan 1809; recorded: pg 32

ROBISON, Thomas - Huntington Twp. Wife: Jane; children: Elenor, David, Sarah, Andrew, Thomas, Martha wife of Jonathan BOWER, John William, Leonard, Hannah (deceased), Mary (deceased), Samuel; executors: son-in-law Jonathan BOWER, Edward HUTTON; witnesses: Abraham BOWER, Philip GROUP, Joseph PILKINGTON; written: 11 Dec 1809; probate: 5 Feb 1811; recorded: pg 137

ROSS, James - Straban Twp., weak. Nieces and nephew: Elenor ROSS daughter of Alice MCEHENEY, David ROSS, Elenor, Isabel and Jane of brother David; executors: brother David, Richard BROWN; witnesses: Jacob CASSATT, Philip GRAFT, John KING; written: 21 Feb 1800; probate: 10 Jun 1809; recorded: pg 54

WILL BOOK B

ROSS, John - Franklin Twp., weak. Wife: Sarah; children: Jean wife of Alexander SWENEY, William, Samuel, David, Sarah, John, Sample; mulatto girl Green to wife; bound mustee boy Jem to Samuel; bound mustee boy Bob to Sarah; executors: sons Sample and Samuel; witnesses: William LAIRD, John EDIE, George SHEAKLY; written: 6 Jan 1805; probate: 6 Apr 1805; recorded: pg 52

ROWAN, Henry - Hamiltonban Twp., yeoman. Wife: Jane; children: James, Robert, Jane wife of David WILSON, Alexander, Henry; executors: son James, son-in-law David WILSON; witnesses: Hugh WILSON, Samuel MCCOLLOUGH, John MORROW; written: 10 Feb 1803; probate: 17 Nov 1809; recorded: pg 1

RUMMEL, George - Straban Twp., weak. Children: Suffia wife of Jacob MAYE(?), Jacob, George, Peter, Christian, John, Catharine wife of Conrad LOURE, Elizabeth wife of John LOURE, Susanna wife of Henry ASHBAUGH, Barbara wife of Christian CULP, Mary wife of Philip SNELL, Henry; executors: son Peter, son-in-law Christian CULP; witnesses: yeoman: John SEMPLE, William GILLELAND; written: 15 Feb 1808; probate: 29 Nov 1810; recorded: pg 100

SANDERS, Peter - Hamiltonban Twp., sick. Wife: Susanna; children: Anthony, Peter, Jacob, Michael, John, Henry, George, Adam, Charles, Margaret, Martha; executors: sons Anthony, Peter; witnesses: David PFOUTZ, Christian HUSHEY; written: 18 Jan 1817; probate: 27 Mar 1817; recorded: pg 517

SCHANE, Joseph - Conewago Twp., carpenter, weak. Wife: Elizabeth; children: Joseph, Anthony, George; executors: wife, George STINE; witnesses: George STEIN, Simon COPPONHAFER, John AULABAUGH; written: 9 Mar 1811; probate: 6 Apr 1811; recorded: pg 152

SCHRIVER, Phillip - Reading Twp. Wife: not named, to still receive her yearly dowry which is now coming from Henry CHRONISTER Sr.; children: sons and daughters, names Elizabeth, Henry; executors: Henry SCHRIVER, John MEIL(?); witnesses: Isaac GRIST, Nicholas MILLER, David CHRONISTER; written: 31 Dec 1813; probate: 5 Jun 1815; recorded: pg 416

SELL, Jacob - Gettysburg, merchant. Wife: Mary Elizabeth; children: Mary, Catherine, Henry, John, Jacob, Elizabeth wife of George ELBERT; executors: sons John, Henry; witnesses: James GETTYS, William MAXWELL, John LASHELL; written: 31 Mar 1812; probate: 13 Oct 1813; recorded: pg 266

SHEAFFER, Mary - Reading Twp., widow of John, weak. Children: Elizabeth wife of Samuel GRABLE, Mary wife of Jacob HILDEBRAND, Daniel, Margaret wife of Samuel WEIDLE, Catherina, Susanah, Lydia, Nancy, John, Julian; father: Tobias REAM whose will was proved in Lancaster Co.; executor: John HILDEBRAND; witnesses: Jacob HILDEBRAND, Daniel SHEAFFER; written: 15 Feb 1812; probate: 23 Mar 1812; recorded: pg 179

SHEKELY, George - Franklin Twp. Wife: Margaret, to receive Negro Barbara; children: William, Robert, Margaret wife of John HAMILTON, Ann wife of William LAWIMER(?), Nancy; executors: son William, John EDIE; witnesses: Adam BLACK, John STONER, Moses JENKINS; written: 10 Jun 1811; probate: 18 Jun 1812; recorded: pg 196

SHRIVER, Lewis - Cumberland Twp., sick. Wife: Mary; children: Jacob, ELizabeth wife of Benjamin ROUDSING(?), Barbara wife of John GLASS, Frederick William, Mary wife of -- ROTROUGHT, Susanna widow of Jacob MYERS, George Lewis, Catherine wife of John BEAR (he abandoned her), Anna, Christian, Sarah, Rachel; son George Lewis to receive land in Columbiana Co., Ohio; executors: sons George Lewis, Christian (renounced); witnesses: Samuel WITHROW, Robert BRECKENRIDGE, Alexander RUSSELL; written: 4 Jul 1815; probate: 22 Jul 1815; recorded: pg 420

SHROCK, Charity - Mt Pleasant Twp., weak. Children: Magdelene, Phillip, Elizabeth wife of Jacob SHAW(?), Catherine wife of Christian FEESSE(?), Barbara wife of John HEINER(?); executor: daughter Magdelene; witnesses:

WILL BOOK B

Abraham ALBERT, Daniel SLAGLE; written: 24 Sep 1814; probate: 12 Aug 1815; recorded: pg 423
   SIDSINGER, Barbara - Huntington Twp., weak. Children: Henry, Leonard, Mary, Margaret, Sarah, Barbara wife of Benjamin ASPER, Elizabeth wife of John MUNTORF; grandchildren(?) three children of Samuel RUSS(?) by his first wife to have their mother's share; executors: son-in-law Benjamin ASPER, Burkhart WARNER; witnesses: George MORTORFF, John LEAS; written: 19 Dec 1810; probate: 7 Jan 1811; recorded: pg 103
   SIEF, Christian - Straban Twp. Wife: Elizabeth; bequest to Christian, Elizabeth, Mary, Philip, Peter, Susanne, John children of Philip THOMAS Sr.; executor: Christian THOMAS; witnesses: William CASHMAN, Christian ESSIG; written: 9 Feb 1814; probate: 15 Feb 1816; recorded: pg 458
   SILLIK, Thomas - Menallen Twp., weak. Children: Hamilton, Mary, Agness, Margaret, Rachel, Emma, Thomas; executors: William GILLILAND, George HICKENLUBER; witnesses: John NEELY, John GILLILAND, William GILLILAND Jr.; written: 8 Jun 1814; probate: 1 May 1815; recorded: pg 408
   SIMUND, Henry - Franklin Twp., old and infirm. Wife: Elizabeth; children: Henry, Elizabeth wife of Andrew HUSTON, Nancy wife of Joseph TURNER, Mary Ann, Andrew, Reginah wife of Bernhard GILBERT; executor: wife; witnesses: Michael CROWEL, John ARENDT; written: 30 May 1814; probate: 25 Jun 1816; recorded: pg 484
   SLAGLE, Henry - Berwick Twp., advanced in age. Wife: Dorothy; children: Elizabeth, Michael, James, Christina BAHN, Cathrina NACE, Margaret WINROTT, Nancy WINROTT, Henry; grandchildren of Mary WOLF; executors: son Michael, sons-in-law George NACE, Jacob WINROTT; witnesses: Joseph SNEERINGER, David SLAGLE; written: 20 Jan 1811; probate: 23 Feb 1811; recorded: pg 141
   SLAGLE, Jacob - Berwick Twp., yeoman. Wife: Eve Margaret very ill; children: Jacob, George, Margaret wife of John STABB, Catharine wife of Jacob KLAPSADDLE, Elizabeth, Mary; executors: David and Michael SLAGLE; witnesses: Jacob SNIDER, Henry MICHAEL, John L. HINKLE; written: 10 Feb 1815; probate: 5 Nov 1816; recorded: pg 501
   SLENCE, Philip - Mt Pleasant Twp. Children: Mary wife of John HEAGY, Catherine wife of Andrew POLLY, Jacob, Hannah wife of George HEAGY, John (deceased), Sally wife of Jacob ---rine, Margaret wife of John ASHBAUGH; executors: son Jacob, Gilbert BRINKERHOOF; witnesses: George and Betsy BRINKERHOFF; written: 3 Dec 1814; probate: 22 Feb 1816; recorded: pg 461
   SNEERINGER, Julyana - Germany Twp., weak. Children: John, Margaret wife of Adam KELLENBERGER; bequest to four children of step daughter-in-law, widow of Lourence SNEERINGER; bequest to William, Samuel, David and Polly children of Jacob SHORPS and his second wife Christine; bequest to Peter, John, Jacob, Susanna, Margaret and Elizabeth children of Christian and Catherine ECKENROTT; bequest to Margaret wife of John SEEKFRIET; executor: nephew Joseph SNEERINGER; witnesses: William SLYDER, Jacob KITSMILLER, Adam KELLENBERGER; codicil 30 Aug 1813 revoked bequest to step daughter-in-law and her children and changed Susana ECKENROTT's bequest to her daughter Mary Ann ECKENROTT; written: 27 Jul 1813; probate: 26 Oct 1813; recorded: pg 269
   STEWART, John - Menallen Twp., weak. Children: Sally, David, Martha, Charles, John and a daughter wife of Moses JENKINS; grandchildren: Martha, Libby, Moses, Anna Maria and Fanny JENKINS, Matta Maria STEWART, Peggy Flemming STEWART, Sally Eliza STEWART, John of David, Tilly Levina STEWART, Charlotte Jane and Nancy STEWART; executors: sons Charles, John; witnesses: John WRIGHT Jr., Nathan WRIGHT, William MCGREW; written: 26 Apr 1814; probate: 28 May 1814; recorded: pg 322

WILL BOOK B

STEWART, Libby - Menallen Twp., weak. Sister: Martha; bequest to Maria DIXON; executors: brother David STEWART, George WILSON; witnesses: John WRIGHT Jr., Andrew WRAY; written: 7 Feb 1816; probate: 25 Mar 1816; recorded: pg 463
STEWART, Martha - Menallen Twp., weak. Siblings: Charles, David; bequest to Mariah DIXON, niece Martha Maria of David; bequest to Martha, Libby, Moses, Ann Maria, Fanny children of sister Mary Ann JENKINS (deceased); executors: brother Charles, John WRIGHT Jr.; witnesses: George WILFORD, Andrew WRAY; written: 9 Oct 1816; probate: 15 Nov 1816; recorded: pg 504
STEWART, Robert - Liberty Twp., farmer. Children: William, John, James, David, Joseph, Robert, Mary CUNNINGHAM, Jane wife of John STEWART, Sarah, Rebecca; executors: son Robert, son-in-law John STEWART; witnesses: William BIGHAM, James CUNNINGHAM; written: 9 Oct 1811; probate: 13 Nov 1811; recorded: pg 173
STEWART, William - Cumberland Twp., farmer, weak. Children: James, Mary (deceased) wife of Robert GIBSON (of Kentucky), Elizabeth wife of Joseph WALKER, Jane wife of John STEWART; grandchildren: William, David and Margaret of James, William, Jane, Mary, John, Joseph, James S., Robert, Samuel and youngest daughter presumed to be named Elizabeth all of Mary, William of Elizabeth; Negro Rachel, till 34 years old, to Elizabeth and Jane; tombstones for self and deceased wife Jane; executors: sons-in-law Joseph WALKER, John STEWART; witnesses: Quinten and Isaac ARMSTRONG, John MORROW; written: 29 May 1806; probate: 7 May 1808; recorded: pg 10
STIGERS, John - Berwick Twp., sick. Wife: Betsy; children: Joseph, George, Charles, Elizabeth (in convent of Sisters of St. Joseph, Frederick Co., Md.), Matilda, John, Matthias, Ann, Mary, Henry, Francis; bequest to Rev. DEBARTH at Roman Catholic Church, Conewago; land in Harrison Co., Va., houses in Baltimore; executors: son George, Samuel LILLY; witnesses: Nicholas WALTER, Thomas J. HICKLEY, Michael SLAGLE; written: 31 Jan 1813; probate: 15 Feb 1813; recorded: pg 216
STORM, Joseph - Conewago Twp., yeoman, very sick. Wife: Margaret; children: Anna Mary widow of Paul BAUMGARDNER, Lavina wife of Adam LONG, Margaret wife of Engelhard SMALL, James, Susanna, Anthony; bequest to BAUMGARDNER grandchildren, naming Jacob; executors: son James, son-in-law Adam LONG; witnesses: John MILLER, Anthony GRICHTIN, John AULEBAUGH; written: 5 Jan 1815; probate: 27 Jan 1815; recorded: pg 370
SWARTZ, Martin - Conewago Twp., very sick. Wife: Catharine; children mentioned; executors: Nicholas GINTER, Abraham KAGY; witnesses: Joseph HILBERADT, John AULABAUGH; written: 2 Feb 1817; probate: 1 Mar 1817; recorded: pg 515
SWENEY, James - Cumberland Twp. Wife: Elisabeth; children: Miles, Andrew, Polly, James, John, Harvey; land in Mercer Co., Pa.; executors: William MCPHERSON, John MCCONAUGHY; witnesses: Alexander COBEAN, David EDIE; written: 3 Sep 1813; probate: 13 Jan 1814; recorded: pg 285
SWIGART, Abraham - town of Berlin. Wife: Eloner; children: John, Mary wife of Martin SMITH, Nancy wife of Jacob BARGOLD(?), James, Sally, Elizabeth, Catherine, Eloner, Love; executors: Abraham ARNOLD, Mathias MUMMERT, both renounced; witnesses: Christian PICKING, Samuel FAHNESTOCK; written: 1 Feb 1814; probate: 21 Mar 1814; Abraham ARNOLD, Abraham TRIMMER named admins; recorded: pg 297
THOMAS, Abel - Menallen Twp., weak. Wife: Eleanor; children: Rebeckah wife of George ALISON(?), Lydia wife of Daniel RICKARD, Jacob, Abner, Rachel wife of William WRIGHT, Eli, Joseph; executors: sons Eli, Joseph; witnesses: Isaac THOMAS, George WILSON; written: 19 Nov 1814; probate: 30 Mar 1816; recorded: pg 466

WILL BOOK B

THOMPSON, Andrew - Huntington Twp., weak. Wife: Jane; children: Mary wife of Robert POLLOCK, Elenor wife of George DILL, Sally wife of Samuel CAMPBELL, Margaret, Jane, Anna wife of William GODFREY, Elizabeth, William; executor: son William; witnesses: Levy MILLER, David MUNDORFF; written: 2 Mar 1811; probate: 4 May 1811; recorded: pg 157

THOMPSON, Joseph - Mt Pleasant Twp., very sick. Children: James, Joseph, John, others(?); executors: sons Joseph, John; witnesses: Isaac ROBISON, Jacob GUNKEL, Aaron TORRENCE; written: 18 Apr 1812; probate: 20 May 1812; recorded: pg 192

TOMLINSON, Benjamin Sr. - Latimore Twp., weak. Sons: Joseph, Benjamin; executors: David GRIEST, Peter BOWER; witnesses: John GRIEST, Samuel COMLY; written: 26 Jan 1817; probate: 29 Jan 1817; recorded: pg 513

TRONE, John - Franklin Twp. Wife: Catharina; children: Jacob, Magdalena, Samuel, John, Anna; friend Isaac BOYER appointed guardian of Ester and Eve STOCKSLAGER, minor children of late John STOCKSLAGER; executors: brother George, John ARENDT; witnesses; Henry HOOVER, David FLECK, George ARENDT; written: 21 Jan 1815; probate: 25 Feb 1815; recorded: pg 387

TUCKER, Tempest - Berwick Twp. Wife: Mary; children: Elizabeth MCCURDY, Anne (deceased) wife of Caleb BALES, Thomas, James; exeuctors: sons Thomas, James; witnesses: William GINKINS, Henry WALES; written: 9 Dec 1812; probate: 31 May 1816; recorded: pg 475

WALKER, James - Tyrone Twp., weak. Wife: Jane; children: James, William, Gennet MCCREARY, Ann, Widner(daughter), Elizabeth ORR, Mary JOHNTON; grandchildren: James and John of William, Ann GARNER, James WITNER of Rosey; executors: nephew Andrew WALKER of William, William MALES; witnesses: George, Sarah and John DELAP; written: 20 Jun 1808; probate: 17 Nov 1810; recorded: pg 93

WALTMAN, Henry - McSherrystown, weaver, weak. Wife: Christina; children: Salome, Christian, Henry, John, Joseph; executors: wife and son Henry; witnesses: David MAILHORN, David MELLINGER; written: 22 Mar 1811; probate: 20 Apr 1811; recorded: pg 155

WAUGH, David - Liberty Twp., weak. Children: William, daughter wife of John KYLE, Polly wife of Robert MCJIMSEY, Peggy wife of Zaccheus PATTERSON, Nancy wife of James KYLE, John, Jane wife of Rev. John COULTER, Sally wife of Rev. John HUTCHESON, Annie wife of John MCCRACKEN; Negro Dolly and yellow girl Phebe to Annie; grandson David PATTERSON to receive Negro Jack; executor: John KERR (renounced); witnesses: Robert MCCRACKEN, Robert SLEMMENS Jr., Joseph MCGINLEY; written: 14 Oct 1816; probate: 4 Dec 1816; recorded: pg 505

WEAKLY, William - Reading Twp., weak. Children: James, Polly, Esther MAXWELL, Rebekah CRAIGHEAD, Martha, others; grandchildren: William, Jennet and Nancy JONES, Martha, Jennet, Elisa, Maria MCGREW, Elliot MAXWELL; great grandson: William DICKS; Negro Bess to Polly; executors: sons-in-law Thomas CRAIGHEAD, Dr. John B. ARNOLD; witnesses: James and Allen ROBINETTE; written: 2 Jul 1813; probate: 6 Sep 1813; recorded: pg 260

WEAVER, Nicholas - Huntington Twp., weak. Bequest to John FRAZIER, children of Levi MILLER, children of Eli MILLER, children of Phebe MINICH by George MINICH; executors: Nicholas WIREMAN, Stephen SPEAKMAN; witnesses: Moses VANSCOYCE, Isaac PEARSON; written: 14 Mar 1814; probate: 26 Mar 1814; recorded: pg 301

WERTZ, Burkhart - Straban Twp., innkeeper, sick. Wife: Catharine; children: William, Peter, John, Elizabeth, Magdalena; mother Jane; father Jacob (deceased); executors: Nicholas DETRICK, George SMYSER; witnesses: William KING Sr., Jacob EYSTER; written: 7 Mar 1811; probate: 2 Apr 1811; recorded: pg 148

WILL BOOK B

WHITE, James - Huntington Twp., sick. Formerly of Carolina; brother: Samuel; mentions Mr. MCCALMOD and Boys of Philadelphia Co., Pa., Robert GETTIS of Charlestown, Moses LEISTER; executor: brother Samuel; witnesses: George ESPY, George SMITH; written: 1 Mar 1812; probate: 26 Apr 1813; recorded: pg 226

WIBLE, Steffen - Straban Twp., weak. Wife: Mary; children: Steffen, John, Joseph, David, Elisabeth, Mary; executors: John WELTY, Henry HOKE; witnesses: Jacob GARETER, Conrod HOKE; written: 18 Aug 1814; codicil written 14 Feb 1815 witnessed by Jacob WERTZ, Moses DEGROFFT; probate: 10 Apr 1815; recorded: pg 401

WILEY, Robert - Huntington Twp. Nephews: James ELIOTT, John and Robert WILEY; bequests to Ann CHAMBERS, Elizabeth wife of George CHAMBERS, Elizabeth wife of Nicholas WIREMAN, shoemaker, and John WILLIAMSON; executors: nephew James ELIOTT, Edward HUTTON; witnesses: Thomas WIREMAN, William PATTERSON; written: 8 Aug 1811; probate: 23 Dec 1811; recorded: pg 175

WILL, Jacob - Conewago Twp., weak. Wife: Elizabeth; children: George, Rachel LITTLE, Elizabeth, Catharine, Sarah, David, Andrew, Jacob, Mary HOPPERT; brother: Andrew; grandchildren: Eve SCHRIVER, Mary of Mary, Sarah and Ebelina of Jacob; land in Mercer Co., Pa.; executors: son George, Andrew SCHRIVER; witnesses: Robert MCILHINNY, John ECKORD, Jacob ECKERT; written: 13 Apr 1812; probate: 12 Nov 1812; recorded: pg 206

WILSON, Benjamin - Menallen Twp. Wife: Sarah; children: George, Ruth wife of James MATHER, Mary, Ealce, Sarah; executors: wife and son George; witnesses: Benjamin HARRIS, John WRIGHT, Jacob KOCH; written: 9 May 1804; probate: 6 Aug 1813; recorded: pg 252

WILSON, Jane - Gettysburg, singlewoman, sick. Child: William Nelson DILL; executor: uncle Hugh DUNWOODY; witnesses: Henry TOPPER, Alexander RUSSELL; written: 24 Mar 1812; probate: 4 Apr 1812; recorded: pg 181

WILSON, Robert - Mt Joy Twp., very weak. Wife: mentioned; children: John, Margaret wife of William STEVENSON, Charles, Mary Ann wife of Thomas DUNWOODY, William, Elizabeth, Sarah, Jane, Esther, Levi, Charlotte, Nancy; executor: son John; witnesses: William DURBORROW, Abdel MCALLISTER, Alexander RUSSELL; written: 4 Mar 1815; probate: 11 Mar 1815; recorded: pg 390

WILSON, Robert - Straban Twp., weak. Wife: Agness; children: Mary wife of Alexander RITCHEY, Sarah wife of Robert LONG, Elizabeth, Agness, William, Thomas, Robert; grandchildren of deceased daughters Ann SCOTTE, Mary PATTERSON; executors: sons Thomas, Robert; witnesses: Andrew ZIEGLER, William GILLELAND; written: 17 Feb 1800; probate: 13 Mar 1814; ZIEGLER proved will at Muskingum Co., Ohio; recorded: pg 468

WINEMILLER, Christopher - Germany Twp., frail. Wife: Elizabeth; children: Adam, Michael, George, Jacob; executors: Ludwick SHERER, David HOOVER; witnesses: Robert MCILHINNY, Samuel BEECHER, Adam GEISELMAN; written: 17 Jul 1812; probate: 5 Mar 1813; recorded: pg 221

WINROTH, Adam Esq. - Petersburg (Littlestown), advanced in age. Sons: John and Jacob; bequest to children of step-daughter Catharine wife of Jacob HOSTETTER Esq.; executors: sons John, Jacob, Andrew SCHRIVER; witnesses: Adam WINTERODE Jr., Benjamin FINK, William MAXWELL; written: 28 Jan 1812; probate: 17 Dec 1813; recorded: pg 279

WOLF, John Sr. - Berwick Twp., farmer, very sick. Wife: Anna Barbara; children: John, Isaac, George, Henry, Elizabeth, Catherina, Nancy, Mary, Jacob, Daniel; executors: wife, son John; witnesses: George NOLL, Tobias KEPNER; written: 15 Dec 1814; probate: 6 Jan 1815; recorded: pg 367

WORK, Robert - Cumberland Twp., sick. Wife: Margaret; daughter: Dorcas; sister: Rachel widow of Adonijah POUNDS; executors: daughter, Isaac ARMSTRONG;

WILL BOOK B

witnesses: Quinten ARMSTRONG, George KERR; written: 10 Feb 1813; probate: 25 Jan 1814; recorded: pg 286

WORST, Jacob - Hanover, York Co., weaver, sick. Wife: Mary; executor: wife; witnesses: Jacob BUCHER, Christian WIRT, Jacob RUDISELL; written: 30 Aug 1804; probate: 9 Nov 1816; recorded: pg 500

YETTS, William - Menallen Twp., weak. Wife: Elisabeth; children: John, William, Simeon, Elisabeth, Mary, Peggy, Daniel, Jonathan, Susannah, Sally; granddaughter: Sally RIFE of Mary; executors: wife, son-in-law Jacob BUSHY; witnesses: George SHALLER, John GILLILAND; written: 20 Nov 1811; probate: 16 Mar 1812; recorded: pg 184

YOUNG, Ann Maria - Mt Pleasant Twp., widow of Frederick. Children: George, Catherine wife of Jacob B---, Baltzer, Magdalena wife of John MYER, Anne Maria wife of -- BRINESHOLD, Elisabeth wife of Frederick BOYER, Barbara wife of George SCHNIDER, Frederick, Peter; Beltzer and John YOUNG guardians of George; executors: Frederick YOUNG, John BRINESHOLD; witnesses: James, Moses Jr. and M. LOCKHART; written: 19 Dec 1808; probate: 20 Dec 1815; recorded: pg 438

YOUNG, Robert - Mt Joy Twp. Children: Robert, John, Mary WILSON, Alexander, James, Agnes; grandchildren: Elizabeth WILSON, Elizabeth YOUNG; executors: son Robert, James WILSON; witnesses: Henry BRINKERHOF, Aaron TORRENCE, William EWING; written: 21 Mar 1808; probate: 11 Aug 1810; recorded: pg 82

ZELL, Peter - Mt Joy Twp. Wife: Esther; sons and daughters including John; executors: sons Barnet, Christian; witnesses: Robert MCILHENNY, Samuel HUNTER, Robert STEWART; written: 9 Feb 1801; probate: 5 Apr 1809; recorded: pg 43

WILL BOOK C

ADAMS, Jacob - Berwick Twp., weak. Wife: Mary; children: Jacob, John, Magdalen, Susana, Rachel; executors: son Jacob, John SMITH; witnesses: Joseph KLUNK, John PECHER, Samuel LILLY; written: 16 Aug 1822; probate: 27 Aug 1822; recorded: pg 261

AGNEW, James - Gettysburg, infirm. Wife: mentioned; children: Betsey, David, James, Rebecca (deceased) wife of Rev. BALDRIDGE, John (deceased), Polly wife of Alexander CALDWELL, Samuel, Martha (deceased) wife of David WILSON; executors: son James son-in-law Alexander CALDWELL; witnesses: John GALLOWAY, Robert HAYES; written: 22 Mar 1825; probate: 14 Apr 1825; recorded: pg 403

AGNEW, Mary - Gettysburg, widow, weak. Children: Elizabeth R., Mary wife of Alexander CALDWELL; grandchildren: Martha Harriet and Rebecca WILSON, Mary Ruth CALDWELL, Elizabeth M. and Mary Ann AGNEW, Mary Jane Ramsey BALDRIDGE; executor: son-in-law Alexander CALDWELL; witnesses: Robert HAYES, John GALLOWAY; written: 15 May 1825; probate: 1 Aug 1825; recorded: pg 420

ALBERT, John - Latimore Twp., farmer, very sick. Children: George, Rebecca, David, Catharine wife of George HERMAN; executors: son George, son-in-law George HERMAN; witnesses: Jacob RORBAUGH, Benjamin BOWER; written: 5 Feb 1819; probate: 29 Mar 1819; recorded: pg 80

ALBERT, John Sr. - Latimore Twp. Wife: Katharine; children: John Jr., Barbara wife of Conrad HEIM, Mary wife of George JACOBS, Margaret wife of Daniel FICKES; stepson: Valentine ECKER(?); executor: son-in-law George JACOBS; witnesses: Philip and Conrad MYERS, Charles KITTLEWELL; written: 1820; probate: 30 Oct 1821; recorded: pg 181

APLEY, Leonard - Tyrone Twp. Children: John, Jacob, Henry, Michael, David, Catharine widow of William CLARK, Elizabeth wife of Silvans DAY, Sarah wife of Thomas GRIFFITH, Margaret wife of Jacob SAWVEL, Susanah; grandchildren: Mary CLARK, John, Jacob, George and Moses WOOLF; executors: John CLINE, Jacob SAWVEL; witnesses: Henry SHRIVER, Nicholas GRIST; written: 3 Mar 1819; probate: 29 Mar 1819; recorded: pg 83

ARNOLD, George - Franklin Twp., sick. Wife: Elizabeth; bequests to unnamed brothers and sisters; executor: John BLOCHER; witnesses: Adam SWOPE, Francis L. KELLY; written: 30 Jul 1822; probate: 17 Jul 1824; recorded: pg 374

ASPER, Margaret - Huntington Twp., widow of Frederick. Children: Mary wife of Levi MILLER, Esther HINKLE (widow), Margaret wife of Henry MILLER, Lydia wife of Philip PORSEL(?), Hannah wife of Jacob ROOP, Sarah widow of Henry PENCE; executors: son-in-law Levi MILLER, John WIERMAN Esq.; witnesses: Charles KITTLEWELL, John MILLER; written: 31 May 1822; probate: 12 Aug 1822; WIERMAN renounced; recorded: pg 252

BARDT, George - Berwick Twp., weak. SIblings: Barbara wife of George LEISER of Ohio, Elizabeth wife of Christian DECK (Abbottstown), Paul in Ohio, Susana, Anna Maria and Magdalena; nphews: George LEISER, George DECK, George of Paul; executor: Adam MYERS; witnesses: Robert MCILWAIN, John L. GUBERNATOR; written: 17 Dec 1818; probate: 12 Apr 1819; recorded: pg 91

BEAKER, John - Hamiltonban Twp., farmer, weak. Wife: Dorothy; children: Peter, Daniel, Andrew, John, Lazarus, Jacob, Katharine wife of John BEAKER, Christiana wife of Frederick WOUTZ(?), Mary wife of John BETTU(?), Nancy, Isabella, Elisabeth; executors: sons John, Peter; witnesses: Alexander MACK, John HINCT; written: 17 May 1813; probate: 25 May 1820; recorded: pg 129

BEAR, Catherine - Franklin Twp., weak, widow of Michael. Executor: Daniel KNOUS; witnesses: Jacob MICKLEY, Valentine FLOHR; written: 11 Dec 1821; probate: 24 Jan 1825; recorded: pg 359

BEASACKER, Nicholas - Franklin Twp. WIfe: Elisabeth; children: Henry, Adam, Catharine, Anna Maria wife of Christian BENNER, Polly wife of Henry

38

WILL BOOK C

WALTER, George, Jacob; grandchildren: Sarah, Mary, Catharine and John WALTER children of Eve (decased) and John WALTER; executors: sons Jacob, Henry; witnesses: Valentine FLORE, Alexander RUSSELL; written: not recorded but witnessed 17 Dec 1813; probate: 10 Jun 1822; recorded: pg 220

BENDER, Conrad - Menallen Twp., weak. Children: Jacob, Henry, Elisabeth WALHEY, Mary WIREMAN, Catharine, Susanah SCHLOSSER, Sophia BAISORE; executors: sons Jacob, Henry; witnesses: Christian RICE, William B. and George WILSON; written: 30 Jan 1823; probate: 6 Nov 1823; recorded: pg 336

BERCAW, Abraham - Straban Twp., sick. Children: Cornelius, John, Abraham, Sally wife of George STOTTER(?), Ann wife of Stephen KITCHEN, Peggy wife of James ALLEN, daughter wife of David DEMAREE, Magdaline wife of Garrett BRINKERHOFF; executors: sons John, Abraham; witnesses: Cornelius LOTT, Abraham KING, George VANDIKE; written: 23 Mar 1824; probate: 25 Jul 1825; recorded: pg 416

BERCAW, George - Straban Twp., sick. Wife: Nelly; children: George, Polly wife of Garret VANARSDAL, Margaret wife of Isaac MANFORT, John, William, Abraham; executors: sons William, Abraham, brother-in-law Cornelius LOTT; witnesses: Isaac BERCAW, John BRINKERHOFF; written: 12 May 1819; probate: 5(?) Jun 1819; recorded: pg 96

BERCAW, Peter Sr. - Mt Joy Twp. Children: George, Joshua, William, Margaret wife of William CROWNOVER, Hannah wife of John KITCHEN; grandchildren: Hannah and Margaret of Isaac, Samuel BERCAW; executors: son George, son-in-law John KITCHEN; witnesses: Andrew LITTLE Jr. Esq., Cornelius LOTT Jr.; written: 20 Jun 1822; probate: 20 Oct 1823; recorded: pg 327

BOWER, Peter Sr. - Latimore Twp. Wife: Mary; children: Nichol(?) PUZEL(?)(daughter), Abraham, Peter, Rachel GRIBLE(?), Hannah, Joshua (deceased); executors: son Peter, Daniel GREIST; witnesses: Andrew LABAUGH, Joel GARRETSON; written: 24 Jun 1816; probate: 24 Nov 1820; recorded: pg 148

BOWERS, Stephen - Latimore Twp., sick. Wife: Mary; son: Jonas; parents mentioned; executor: Joseph BOWER (renounced); witnesses: George HERMAN Jr., Jacob CHRIST; written: 6 May 1824; probate: 29 May 1824; Peter DETTER named administrator; recorded: pg 367

BOYD, Archibald - Cumberland Twp., sick. Wife: Isabella; children: James and six unnamed daughters; granddaughters: Sarah and Isabella of John CROSS; executor: David WILLS; witnesses: David FLETCHER, John MCCLANAHAN; written: 15 Mar 1825; probate: 25 Apr 1825; recorded: pg 407

BRACKENRIDGE, Robert - Liberty Twp. Wife and children metnioned; uncle: Robert BRACKENRIDGE; executors: father William, Robert L. GRIER; witnesses: Peter WICKERT, Samuel WITHEROW; written: 22 Jun 1821; probate: 16 Jul 1821; recorded: pg 173

BRINKERHOFF, George - Straban Twp., sick. Wife: Eidie; children: young; executors: father John, Peter HULICK; witnesses: John SHRIVER, Hezekiah VANORSDOL; written: 20 Jul 1822; probate: 2 Sep 1822; recorded: pg 263

BRINKERHOFF, Gilbert - Mt Pleasant Twp., sick. Wife: Elisabeth; children: George, Cornelius, Martinah, Magdalanah, Charity, Elizabeth; grandson: Peter BERCAW; executors: sons George, Cornelius; witnesses: William THOMPSON, Hezekiah BRINKERHOFF; written: 12 Aug 1821; probate: 1 Sep 1821; recorded: pg 174

BRITT, Adam - Conewago Twp., advanced in age. Estate to Rev. Franciscus NEAL at the College of Georgetown; executor: Rev. Lewis DEBARTH; witnesses: Joseph SNEERINGER, Samuel LILLY; written: 13 no month 1814; probate: 16 Jul 1822; recorded: pg 240

WILL BOOK C

BROWN, James Fulford - Adams Co., weak. Child: Sarah Ann; executors: Dr. John B. ARNOLD, Christian PICKING; witnesses: Charles BLISH, Nathan WEBB, John SLEE; written: 12 Oct 1817; probate: 25 Oct 1817; recorded: pg 8

BUSHMAN, Henry - Cumberland Twp., weak. Children: Mary MILLER, Jacob, John, Andrew, Betsy DEGROFF; executors: son Jacob, son-in-law Michael MILLER; witnesses: Abraham and Margaret LINAH, Benjamin WORKMAN; written: 22 Sep 1818; probate: 31 Dec 1822; recorded: pg 289

CAMPBELL, Margaret - Straban Twp., weak. Niece: Anna wife of Josiah COUTLER; executor: Moses JENKINS; witnesses: Henry BRINKERHOOF, Jacob KEEFHAVER; written: 20 Feb 1824; probate: 30 Apr 1824; recorded: pg 365

CASHMAN, George - Straban Twp., weak. Wife: Eve; children: John, George, William, Polly, CHristina; executors: sons John, George; witnesses: John DIXON, Christian CASHMAN, John YEAGY; written: 6 Jul 1822; probate: 14 Aug 1822; recorded: pg 257

CASSAT, David - Adams Co. Children: Francis (deceased - children to receive land in New York State), David, Peter (deceased with two children), Denis (deceased with two children), Jacob, Idah wife of George BRINKERHOOF, Margaret, Mary wife of Peter HULICK; executors: son Jacob, son-in-law Peter HULICK; witnesses: Abraham KING, Daniel C. ARNOLD; written: 1822; probate: 24 Jan 1824; recorded: pg 348

CHAMBERLAIN, Lewis - Franklin Twp., sick. Wife: Rachel; children: Isaac, David, Joseph, Charlotte wife of Samuel EAKINS, Mary; granddaughters: Hannah and Rebecca of John; bequest to Joseph KENDEL son of John; executors: son David, Jacob COVER; witnesses: John ROBINSON, Elijah SEABROOK, D. MIDDLECOFF; written: 6 Feb 1825; probate: 31 Mar 1825; recorded: pg 398

CHAMBERLIN, Clayton - Franklin Twp., sick. Children: Amelia wife of Elijah SEABROOKE, Maria, Nelly widow of George MCGLAUGHLIN, Joseph, Lewis, David, John; monies due from New Jersey; executors: son Joseph, brother Lewis; witnesses: Christian DITTENHEFER, Samuel MOORE, Abram RUSSELL Esq.; written: 8 Feb 1819; probate: 4 Mar 1819; recorded: pg 74

CHAMBERLIN, James - Reading Twp., unwell. Wife: Ann; children: mentioned; executors: sons Jeremiah and John, John MCCONAUGHEY Esq.; witnesses: Rogers KINYON(?), William PATTERSON; written: 17 Jan 1819; probate: 23 Feb 1819; recorded: pg 72

COLE, Michael - Reading Twp. Wife: Elizabeth's will dated 14 Oct 1807 probated 7 Dec 1807 to be held in full force; children: mentioned only Michael named; bequest to Roman Catholic Church on Little Conewago Creek; executor: son Michael; witnesses: William PATTERSON, Simon PECHER; written: 18 Aug 1808; probate: 8 Apr 1822; signed as Johan Michal COLE; recorded: pg 260

COLLINS, John - Huntington Twp., weak. Wife: Mary; children: John, Ann wife of John ROSS, Sarah, Elizabeth, Mary, Rebekah; executors: son John, Nicholas WIREMAN; witnesses: Nicholas WIREMAN Sr., Samuel KENNEDAY; written: 27 Mar 1811; probate: 7 Apr 1819; recorded: pg 87

COOK, Susanna - Huntington Twp., sick. Daughter: Julian; bequest to Eliza WALKER; executors: James and Allen ROBINETTE; witnesses: Peter DEEMER, Thomas JOHN; written: 2 Oct 1824; probate: 19 Oct 1824; recorded: pg 379

COOPER, Hannah - Gettysburg, widow. Children: Margaret wife of William WALKER, Matilda wife of Samuel HUNTER, John M.; grandson: John Mercer TEST; executor: brother-in-law William STEEPLE/STAPELS, Reisterstown, Md.; witnesses: Robert W. WILSON, Alexander RUSSELL; executor renounced in favor of Hannah's daughters; written: 12 Jun 1822; probate: 2 Nov 1822; recorded: pg 279

COOPER, Thomas - Huntington Twp. Wife: Margaret; children: Mary KENNEDY (deceased), Margaret STEPHENS; executors: sons-in-law Samuel KENNEDY, Thomas

40

WILL BOOK C

STEPHENS, and James ROBINETTE, friend; witnesses: Allen and George ROBINETTE; written: 17 May 1821; probate: 25 Feb 1823; recorded: pg 298

COOPER, William - Gettysburg. Wife: Sarah; children: John, Ann ODLE, Thomas J., William M., Nancy, Sample, Mary, Franklin; Negro woman Peg; executors: sons Thomas, William; witnesses: John F. MCFARLANE, J. MCGONAUGHY; written: 2 May 1818; probate: 10 Oct 1818; recorded: pg 54

COSHUN, John - Adams Co., sick. Wife: Hannah; children: Joseph, John, William, Katharine wife of David CHAMBERLAIN, Betsey, Rebecka, Jane, Anna, Emelia, Maria; executors: sons Joseph, John; witnesses: Aaron TORRENCE, Garret CROWNOVER, James DAUGHERTY; written: 14 Apr 1821; probate: 24 Apr 1821; recorded: pg 162

CROLEY, John - Mt Pleasant Twp., sick. Wife: mentioned, now in County Cork, Parrish of Dunnahmore near Glabrighkelly; bequest to Rev. James COMISKY, Philadelphia; executor: Samuel LILLY; witnesses: Edward RILEY, Samuel BRADY; written: 24 Oct 1823; probate: 10 Nov 1823; recorded: pg 339

CROWNOVER, John Jr. - Mt Pleasant Twp., weak. Wife: Mary; son: David; executors: wife's brother David CHAMBERLIN, Garret CROWNOVER; witnesses: Cornelius LOTT, Hannah COSHUN; written: 29 Aug 1820; probate: 26 Nov 1820; recorded: pg 146

CRYSHER, Susanna - Mt Pleasant Twp., sick. Children: Mary, Catharina, Susannah, Daniel, Jacob; executor: son Daniel; witnesses: Phil. WOLF, Andrew WITT, John SHEELY/SCHELIE; written: 25 Jun 1824; probate: 8 Oct 1825; recorded: pg 430

CUNNINGHAM, James - Berlin Twp., unwell. Siblings: John, Martha; bequest to children of Robert COOK and Adam SWARTZ; executors: Robert COOK, David BRENISON; witnesses: Adam SWARTZ, William PATTERSON; written: 27 Jul 1814; probate: 7 Nov 1816; will established by verdict of jury 13 Jan 1816 in Adams County Court of Common Pleas; recorded: pg 60

CUNNINGHAM, Robert - Liberty Twp., yeoman. Wife: Martha; children: John, Betsey wife of Samuel COBEAN, James; grandchildren: Samuel, Matty of John; bequest to Betsey AGNEW; bequest to daughter-in-law Polly widow of son David; executors: son James, son-in-law Samuel COBEAN; witnesses: James MCCLEARY, John HILL, Hugh BIGHAM; written: 11 Jul 1814; probate: 19 Sep 1823; recorded: pg 322

DAY, Silvanis Sr. - Latimore Twp., weak. Wife: Mary; children: Silvanis, Nelson, others; executors: son Silvanis, James ROBINETTE; witnesses: George and Jacob MYERS; written: 1 Aug 1822; probate: 17 Nov 1823; recorded: pg 340

DEARDOFF, Isaac - Latimore Twp. Wife: Sarah; children: Anne, Elizabeth, Sarah, Christian, Mary, Susanah, Catharine, George, Hannah; grandchildren: Joseph DIEHL, Sarah and Hannah FUNK; executors: son George, James ROBINETTE; witnesses: Jacob LEVINSTON, George ROBINETTE; written: 6 Feb 1822; probate: 12 Sep 1823; recorded: pg 316

DEARDORFF, Anthony - Reading Twp., unwell. Wife: Sarah; children: Sarah wife of John ---, Elizabeth wife of Jacob ROUDEBUSH, Mary wife of John ---, Peter, Anthony, Joseph, Samuel, Christina wife of John GUNKLE, Polly, Hannah (note: Elizabeth, Sarah and Mary apparently to a first wife); executors: Daniel LONENACHER, William PATTERSON; witnesses: John GOLDEN, Henry MEYRS; written: 22 May 1818; probate: 9 Jan 1819; recorded: pg 37

DELAP, John - Tyrone Twp., weak. Wife: Catharine; children: George, John, Leonard, William, Sarah, Ruth wife of Jacob SCHRIVER, Mary; grandson: Eneas NICKEL; executors: sons George, Leonard, John; witnesses: William B. MCGREW, Daniel LEASE; written: 22 Jul 1822; probate: 13 Aug 1822; recorded: pg 254

WILL BOOK C

DELAP, Sarah - Tyrone Twp., weak. Mother: Catherine DELAP; siblings: George, John, Leonard, William, Rebeccah SUMMERS, Ruth SCHRIVER, Mary; nephews and nieces: Eneas NICKEL, John of Leonard, Sarah of John, Ruth SUMMERS, John SCHRIVER of Jacob; executor: brother Leonad DELAP; witnesses: William B. MCGREW, Mary SMITH; written: 9 Feb 1824; probate: 24 Feb 1824; recorded: pg 353

DICH, Thomas - Hamiltonban Twp., weak. Wife: Mary; nephew: Robert R. CALVIN; executor: William MC---; witnesses: James MCRESSON Jr., Samuel HUTCHESON, William MCMILLEN Jr.; written: 6 Nov 1818; probate: 28 Dec 1819; recorded: pg 104

DICKSON, Wilhelmina - Huntington Twp., weak. Mother: Sinor DICKSON; siblings: Margaret, Ann M., Samuel; executors: Clement STUDEBAKER, Robert MCILHENNY Jr.; witnesses: William B. MCGREW, Robert MCILHENNY; written: 20 Jul 1822; probate: 26 Jul 1822; STUDEBAKER renounced; recorded: pg 245

DIEL, Charles - Adams Co. Children: George, Jacob, Eve ROBISON; land in Baltimore, Md., and Columbiana Co., Ohio; executors: son Jacob, Peter WALTER; witnesses: Robert MCILHENNY, Sebastian WEAVER, Jacob ELBERT; written: 15 May 1812; probate: 22 Nov 1820; recorded: Book E, pg 209 when Register of Wills found that the will had not previously been recorded.

DOBBIN, Alexander - Gettysburg, sick. Siblings: Daniel, James, Matthew, Isabella EDIE; executor: Walter SMITH; witnesses: Robert GOLDEN, Sampson S. KING; written: 12 Oct 1822; probate: 17 Oct 1822; recorded: pg 278

DOBBIN, Mary - Cumberland Twp., singlewoman. Siblings: Matthew, James, Alexander, Daniel, Isabella EDIE; executors to buy five pair of marble head and foot gravestones at Baltimore, Md. and set at graves of deceased father, mother, brothers William and Joseph and her grave; executors: brothers Alexander and Matthew; witnesses: Hugh SCOTT, Samuel MCFARLANE, Alexander RUSSELL; written: 25 Mar 1820; probate: 18 Apr 1820; recorded: pg 126

DOBBIN, Mary - Adams County, weak. Children: Smith, John, Robert and Gibson AGNEW, Martha LASHELLS, Rebecca HAYS, Mary REED; stepchildren: Mathew DOBBIN, Isabella EDIE; grandchildren: John RAMSEY, Mary MCKNITT daughter of granddaughter Mary wife of James MCKNITT of Tennessee, David, Mary Jane, Rebecca, Ann Eliza and "another daughter whose name I don't recollect" and John AGNEW, children of son John AGNEW, Susan, David Agnew, Alexander Hamilton, Mary Ann, Rebecca Eliza, John Franklin, Martha Helen and Elizabeth Mable HAYES children of Robert and daughter Rebecca HAYES, Mary Ann, William, Harriet Rebecca, David and Samuel children of Samuel M. and daughter Mary REED; bequest to John LASHELLS Esq., husband of Martha; tombstones to be placed at graves of first husband David AGNEW, her own, daughter Rebecca HAYES, son James, all lying in the Lower Marsh Creek graveyard, and at the grave of son James, lying in the Donegal graveyard in Lancaster Co.; executor: John F. MCFARLANE; witnesses: James GRAY, David MCCONAUGHY; written: 9 Feb 1824; probate: 2 Sep 1824; recorded: pg 376

DOUGLASS, James - Cumberland Twp., sick. Wife: Elizabeth; children: Mary, Martha, Jane, William, Anna, Nelly, James, Elizabeth, Margaret; father-in-law William ORR deceased; brother: Thomas deceased; neighbor John STEWART named guardian of James, Elizabeth and Margaret; executors: son William, Alexander COBEAN; witnesses: Mathew LONGWELL, John GALLOWAY, Alexander ROSS; written: 26 Sep 1817; probate: 5 Mar 1818; recorded: pg 24

DUNWOODY, Elisabeth - Gettysburg. Daughter: Elisabeth wife of Joseph VANOSDALLEN; executors: John MAGOSSEN, John GALLOWAY; witnesses: Francis KNOUS, John MCGONAUGHY; written: 5 May 1814; probate: 2 Jul 1824; recorded: pg 370

WILL BOOK C

ECKERT, Jacob - Straban Twp., low state of health. Wife: Elizabeth; children: Jacob, John, Conrad, George, Sarah, Kathrin, and older married children; executors: son Henry, Hugh JACKSON; witnesses: George WALTER, John HORNBERGER; written: 9 Nov 1821; probate: 26 Nov 1821; recorded: pg 198

ELLIOTT, James - Hamiton Twp., weak. Wife: Catharine; children: Robert, John, James, Samuel, Ann, Catherine, Elizabeth; executors: Edward HATTON, Thomas STEPHENS; witnesses: Nicholas WIERMAN, William THOMPSON; written: 20 Jan 1818; probate: 30 Jan 1818; recorded: pg 17

ELLIS, Alexander - Cumberland Twp. Aunt: Jane HALL; bequest to James, John and Samuel E. HALL and Elsie WILLIAMS; executor: John HALL; witnesses: Abraham and Hugh WILSON; written: 6 Apr 1817; probate: 16 May 1817; recorded: pg 3

EPLEY, Peter - Mt Joy Twp., weak. Wife: Anna; children: Henry, Catharina wife of John YEAGY, Elizabeth, Juliana; executor: son-in-law John YEAGY; witnesses: Christian WAMPLER, Jacob HOKE; written: 9 Sep 1812; probate: 23 Jul 1818; recorded: pg 46

ESSICK, Adam - Straban Twp. Wife: Suffia; children: Suffia, Mary, Jacob, Elisabeth wife of Peter CRUM; bequest to John, Christian and Lewis ESSICK; executors: wife, John BRINKERHOFF (renounced); witnesses: George EYSTER, William GILLILAND Sr. and Jr.; written: 20 Dec 1822, signed as Adam ESSIG; probate: 2 Jan 1824; recorded: pg 347

FANESTOCK, Borius - town of Berlin. Wife: Elizabeth; children: Salome wife of Jacob FANESTOCK, Detrich, Iosala(?) wife of Jacob GARDNER, Mary wife of Peter FANESTOCK, Dina wife of Jacob HOUSELL, Benjamin, Daniel, Elizabeth wife of Thomas REED; requested a service be held in Ephrata, Lancaster Co., also after wife's death; executors: son Detrich, sons-in-law Jacob FANESTOCK, Jacob GARDNER; witnesses: Henry FORRY, William PATTERSON; written: 2 Mar 1820; probate: 22 Jul 1820; recorded: 181

FICKES, Abraham - Huntington Twp., weak. Wife: Rosana; children: Jacob, Peggy wife of Jacob WAINBRIGHT, Betsy wife of George MYERS; executor: son Jacob; witnesses: Daniel SHEFFER, John CRONISTER; written: 18 Mar 1820; probate: 5 Apr 1820; recorded: pg 122

FISHER, Conrad - Franklin Twp., weak. Wife: Susan; children: Catharine, Polly, Daniel, Joseph; executors: son Joseph (renounced), Daniel KNOUS; witnesses: Jacob SHROEDER, Dr. Frederick CHARLES; written: 9 Dec 1825; probate: 13 Dec 1825; recorded: pg 437

FLOHR, David - Franklin Twp., sick. Most entries as FLORE. Wife: Salome; children: Matilda and George Mark; executor: brother Valentine; witnesses: Daniel MICKLEY, Peter MARK, Jacob ---; written: 22 Apr 1823; probate: 3 May 1823; recorded: pg 305

FLOHR, Leonard - Franklin Twp. Children: Leonard, Frederick, Valentine, Sarah wife of Daniel MICKLEY, Joseph (deceased), Samuel, David, Daniel, Jacob; grandchildren: John and Joseph of Joseph; executors: son Valentine, son-in-law Daniel MICKLEY; witnesses: Alexander DOBBIN, William S. COBEAN, Alexander RUSSELL; written: 29 Nov 1814; probate: 10 Jan 1821; recorded: pg 151

FRIED, John - Mt Joy Twp. Estate to Barbara SLONECKER, housekeeper of 39 years, then to her children: Barbara wife of August SNYDER, Cathrine, Regina and Adam FRIED; executor: August SNYDER; witnesses: Adam ROHRBAUGH, Martin WELLER, Jacob DEAL; written: 10 Mar 1823; probate: 2 Feb 1824; recorded: pg 350

GARVIN, William - Gettysburg, sick. Children: Nancy wife of Philip SLENTZ(?), John, David, Thomas (deceased), William, Elizabeth, Margaret; executors: sons John, David; witnesses: Walter SMITH, Thomas BREDEN(?), Alexander RUSSELL; written: 5 Feb 1819; probate: 20 Feb 1819; recorded: pg 67

43

WILL BOOK C

GILBERT, Leonard - Straban Twp., sick. Wife: Elizabeth; children: Lydia, Elizabeth, Suffiah, Hannah, Rebecka, Daniel, Catharina wife of Jacob REX, Sally wife of Johathan REASMAN/REAMAN/REMAN; executors: sons-in-law Jacob REX, Johathan REAMAN; witnesses: John DICKSON, John YEAGY, Samuel HOFFMAN; codicils witnesses: George GILBERT, Abraham SHEFFER; codicils dates: 19 Oct 1822, 15 Nov 1822; written: 15 Sep 1822; probate: 14 Dec 1822; recorded: pg 282

GILLMYER, Francis - Frederick Co., Md., sick. Wife: Catherine (with JENKINS penciled in); children: John (land in Morgantown, Va.), Joseph, Francis, Catherine, Jacob, Elizabeth, Sarah, George, Louisa, Mary MILLER; executor: wife; witnesses: William EMMIT, Thomas RADFORD, Daniel M. MOORE; written: 21 Apr 1816; probate: 7 Oct 1823; recorded: pg 363; also Book 1, pg 225 of Frederick Co.; administrative letters granted 20 Apr 1824 to George GROOVER, John HARRET

GODFREY, Hannah - Franklin Twp., widow of William, weak. Sons: Thomas, Charles; bequests to unnamed children of Thomas; granddaughter: Sidney FICKES of Elizabeth FICKES; grandson: James G. OLIVER of Hannah (to receive watch which belonged to his grandfather but now in the hands of Susanna SHELDON now OLIVER); granddaughter: Hannah of Thomas; executors: sons Thomas, Charles; witnesses: Francis and William COULSON; written: 30 May 1819; probate: 12 Aug 1819; recorded: pg 98

GRAHAM, Margaret - Gettysburg, sick. Bequests to niece Elizabeth WILSON wife of Francis KELLY; Sarah REED wife of Elias HUNT; Margaret REED wife of John BARRETT; Martha MALONEY, living in Cincinnati, formerly her apprentice; residue of estate to: William, Charles, James, Ann wife of Andrew WATHER(?), Esther wife of John ADAIR, and Elizabeth wife of William ---, children of deceased sister Esther WILSON; John, Margaret wife of James BARR(?), Susanna and Samuel, children of deceased sister Jane HUNTER; John, Margaret wife of William STEVESON, Charles, Maryan wife of Thomas DUNWOODY, William SMITH, Elizabeth wife of Francis L. KELLY, Sarah wife of William BEREAND, Jane, Esther, Levi and Charlotte, children of sister Mary, widow of Robert WILSON; executor: John ADAIR; witnesses: Henry KING, John and Alexander RUSSELL; written: 21 Jun 1819; probate: 9 Feb 1820; recorded: pg 117

GRAY, James - Gettysburg. Wife: Mary Anne; executor: wife; witnesses: Charles G. MCLEAN, James H. MILLER; written: 27 Jul 1821; probate: 4 Sep 1824; recorded: pg 378

GREENEWALD, Martin - Germany Twp., yeoman, old. Bequest to: Michael KESLER, son of first wife; Susanna, daughter of first wife; wife: Catherine; daughter: Barbara wife of Adam MENCHEY; executors: wife and John SNYDER; witnesses: Martin HELLER, John MILLER; written: 15 Mar 1819; probate: 5 Apr 1819; wife renounced due to age and moving; recorded: pg 85

GREER, James - Tyrone Twp., sick. Brother: William GREER; executor: brother; witnesses: John BRADSHAW, Edward HATTON; written: 28 Jan 1822; probate: 4 Mar 1822; recorded: pg 218

GROFT, John - Adams Co. Wife. mentioned; children: John and Hannah wife of George GILBERT; son to pay debt owed Philip GROFT; executors: son John, son-in-law George GILBERT; witnesses: William and Joseph GILLILAND; written: 11 Sep 1822; probate: 22 Sep 1822; recorded: pg 275

HAMMOND, Mary - Tyrone Twp. Children: James, John, Susanah WIREMAN; bequests to: Harmon, Matilda, Mary and Ruth WIREMAN; grandchildren: Samuel WRIGHT, Elizabeth THOMAS; executor: son John; witnesses: Mary and Finley MCGREW; written: 1 Mar 1817; probate: 2 Jun 1823; recorded: pg 307

HARTMAN, Katharina - Hamilton Twp., singlewoman. Brother: Philip HARTMAN; bequest to poor to be handled by Overseers of the Poor of the Germany

WILL BOOK C

Baptist Church; executor: brother; witnesses: Jacob BIER(?), John SWARTZ, Herman BLOSSER; written: 21 Jan 1819; probate: 23 Nov 1820; recorded: pg 145
    HARTZEL, George - Menallen Twp., weak. Wife: Hannah; children: Henry, Catharina wife of Henry BREAM, Sarah wife of ---, Elizabeth wife of William NEAL, Hannah wife of Philip LONG, Zusanna wife of Henry KOSSER, Mary wife of Jacob BENTZEL, Barbara, George, Philip, John, Leonard, Jacob; executors: sons George, Philip; witnesses: George SMYSER, Leonard YEAGY, Henry SELL; written: 23 Feb 1814; codicil: 8 Feb 1817 daughter Sarah's share to her children: George, Catharine, Samuel and John CONRAD, witnessed by Conrad SMYSER, Henry HOKE; codicil: 6 Jun 1824, son Philip deceased, to be replaced as executor by Henry BREAM, witnessed by Henry HOKE, Jacob ZIEGLER; codicil: 26 Oct 1824, witnessed by Charles F. KEENER, Jacob NULL; probate: 13 Nov 1824; recorded: pg 382
    HATTON, Margaret - Huntington Twp., weak. Bequests: Margaret wife of Thomas COOPER, Margaret C., Deborah C., Mary C., Thomas C., Hatton C., children of Samuel KENADY, Margaret wife of Thomas STEPHENS; executors: Samuel KENADY, Thomas STEPHENS; witnesses: Nicholas GROOP, Thomas COOPER, George JOYCE; written: 6 Dec 1815; probate: 12 Sep 1823; recorded: pg 319
    HEAGEY, john - Mt Joy Twp. Wife: Mary; children: John, Samuel, Philip, Goerge, with bequests to children of daughters Mary (deceased) wife of William EWING; three grandsons: John of John, Philip and George HEAGEY; executors: sons Philip, George; witnesses: David EDIE, Samuel HUTCHISON; written: 1 Dec 1816; probate: 12 Feb 1821; recorded: pg 153
    HEAGY, Jacob - Conewago Twp. Wife: Christina; children: John, Elizabeth wife of Martin KITZMILLER, Joseph, Mary wife of David SHOWALTER, Catherine wife of William GILBERT, George, Jacob (deceased); executors: sons Joseph, George, John L. HINKLE; witnesses: William and Daniel GITT, John HOUCK; written: 24 Jul 1822; probate: 25 Apr 1825; recorded: pg 405
    HECK, Daniel - Cumberland Twp., sick. Children: Daniel, George, Jacob, John, Catharine, Rebecca; executors: son Daniel, George TROSTLE; witnesses: William GREGLOW, James HEAGY, John CARVIN; written: 2 Dec 1824; probate: 25 Dec 1824; recorded: pg 387
    HECKENLUBER, George - Menallen Twp., sick. Wife: Rachel; children: mentioned with only Catharine named; grandchild: Mary BLANKLY; executors: wife, William GILLILAND Sr.; witnesses: Adam PLUMP, P. AUGHINBAUGH; written: 1 Apr 1822; probate: 9 May 1822; recorded: pg 224
    HERSHEY, Joseph - Hamilton Twp. Wife: Barbara; children: Christian, Barbara wife of Jacob BEAR, Elizabeth wife of David HOLLINGER, Susannah, Henry, Anna wife of John RIFE, Nelly JACOBS; mentions Jacob HERSHEY; executor: son Christian; witnesses: John ATTIG, William PATTERSON; written: 25 Dec 1822; probate: 22 Nov 1823; recorded: pg 342
    HODGE, William - Reading Twp., unwell. Executors to buy gravestones for his parents and his grave; bequests: sister wife of Samuel KNOX and her daughter Peggy wife of James MORROW, and to Samuel KNOX, nephew; residue to: John and Samuel KNOX, Peggy MORROW, William, Samuel and Peggy CHAMBERLAIN; executors: James MORROW, William PATTERSON; witnesses: John SHETRONE, David WHITE; written: 6 May 1819; probate: 13 Nov 1821; recorded: pg 192
    HOKE, Conrad - Adams County, declining health. Wife: mentioned; sons: Conrad, John, Jacob; executors: none named or appointed; witnesses: Andrew BUSHMAN, James GUYNN, William KELLY; written: 8 Feb 1822; probate: 30 Apr 1823; recorded: pg 304
    HOKE, John - Hamiltonban Twp., weak. Wife: Julianna; brother: David HOKE; sister: Barbara wife of Arthur BENNETT; father: Bartholomew HOKE (deceased); John, Jacob, Polly, Eliza, David, Kitty children of brother Joseph

WILL BOOK C

HOKE; executors: John MUSSELMAN, John MARSHALL; witnesses: Robert L. and Andrew ANNAN, Joseph MCGINTY; written: 27 May 1825; probate: 27 Sep 1825; recorded: pg 427

HOOFNAGLE, Margaret - Adams Co., widow, sick. Sister: Hottlehency(?); daughter: Maricah wife of Peter BROWN; executor: son-in-law Peter BROWN; witnesses: Anthony WELK, John JONES; written: 5 Apr 1825; probate: 10 Nov 1825; recorded: pg 436

HORNER, Mary - Mt Joy Twp., widow, infirm. Nine children including: William, Andrew, John, Robert, Margaret wife of William FINDLY, Polly wife of Archibald WITHEROW; mentions David HORNER, admin of late husband's estate; executor: son David; witnesses: John GALLOWAY, Andrew GIFFIN, Alexander RUSSELL; written: 5 Dec 1811; probate: 10 Apr 1820; recorded: pg 124

HUFFNAGLE, John Sr. - Germany Twp., yeoman, weak. Wife: Margaret; two children: John and Mary wife of Peter BROWN; executor: brother-in-law Philip BART; witnesses: Frederick CAMP, Adam UMMER; written: 21 Aug 1824; probate: 17 Feb 1825; BART renounced as witnessed by John WIKERT, letters to Peter BROWN; recorded: pg 393

HULL, Nicholas - Berwick Twp. Wife: Anna Eve; children: John, Philip, George, Catharina wife of William OWINGS, Peter; executor: son Peter; witnesses: John NOLL, Tobias KEPNER; written: 9 May 1812; probate: 14 May 1818 when John NOLL's (deceased) signature attested to by George NOLL; recorded: pg 35

HUNTER, Isabella - Mt Joy Twp. Father: Samuel HUNTER (deceased); mother: Margaret HUNTER; newphew: John HUNTER; executor: James BARR; witnesses: Robert, John and Joseph HUNTER; written: 1 Mar 1817; probate: 12 Sep 1817; recorded: pg 5

HUNTER, Joseph - Mt Joy Twp. Children: mentioned; grandchildren: Susanah Jean BERCAW, Joseph son of John HUNTER; executor: son-in-law James BARR; witnesses: Robert MCILHINNY, John ADAIR, John HUNTER; written: 16 Jun 1824; probate: 23 Aug 1825; recorded: pg 425

HUNTER, William - Adams County, sick. Wife: Elizabeth; brother: Alexander; nephews: John, Adam; wife's niece: Jane SHIELDS; "my --- " Joseph HUNTER who resided with him for some years; executor: Samuel MCNAIR; witnesses: John ZIMMERMAN, G. M. EICHELBERGER; written: 23 Aug 1822; probate: 14 Sep 1822; recorded: pg 267

JENKINS, William - Berwick Twp., merchant. Wife: Clemence; children: JoAnna, William, Elisabeth, Hanna Mary; mentions living father; executor: Franics B---, Cumberland Co., Pa.; witnesses: Sebastian KEFER, Tobias KEPNER; written: 9 Jul 1817; probate: 14 Sep 1818; recorded: pg 53

KEARNEY, Martin Joseph - Adams County, sick. Siblings: Nicholas F., John, Ellen, Mary Ann; executor: Eealnor M. KEARNEY; witnesses: Thomas RADFORD, Peter BOYLE, William FURGESON; written: 27 Oct 1818 at Emmitsburg, Md.; probate: 19 Nov 1818; recorded: pg 56

KEEFHAUVER, Nicholas - Conewago Twp., farmer. Wife: Elizabeth; children: Philip, COnrad, Jacob, Peter, Nicholas, Catharine; son-in-law: Anthony FINK; executors: wife, son-in-law; witnesses: Peter and Jacob BRITZHER; written: 5 May 1814; probate: 26 Jan 1818; wife and son-in-law renounced; Michael KITZMILLER, Anthony FINK and Jacob BROTHERS held bound for $14,000; Michael KITZMILLER named admin 24 Mar 1818; recorded: pg 13

KEPLINGER, Hannah - Berwick Twp., widow, very sick. Executor: son Peter; witnesses: Daniel EYSTER, David SLAGLE, John AULABAUGH; written: 14 Mar 1820; probate: 21 May 1819; previous dates are as recorded, the probate date being correct; recorded: pg 95

WILL BOOK C

KIMMEL, Jacob - town of Berlin. Wife: Ann; mentions marriage contract dated 1 Jul 1805; grandchildren: Jacob, Philip, Catharina, Sally, Lydia children of Philip (deceased), Jacob of Samuel (deceased), Elizabeth and Esther WATSON children of unnamed daughter; bequest to John WATSON; daughters: Mary wife of Henry FOX, Catharina wife of Abraham MILEY; executor: Samuel FANESTOCK; witnesses: Daniel FUNDENBURG, Henry FORRY; written: 2 Dec 1813; probate: 16 Dec 1818; FAHNESTOCK renounced; recorded: pg 57

KITZMILLER, George - Conewago Twp. Wife: Christina; children: Michael, Martin, Mary, Margaret, Christina, Rachel, Susannah; Negro men Ritch and William to be freed at his death; Negro woman Winkey to wife and following her death to daughter Rachel or freedom, to be Winkey's choice; executors: son Michael, son-in-law Jacob DEWALT; witnesses: Robert MCILHINNY, Robert JONES, Nathan HENDRICKS, Jacob DELLONE, Peter KEEFHAVER; written: 21 May 1815; probate: 27 Mar 1824; recorded: pg 360

KLINE, John - Mt Pleasant Twp., yeoman, advanced of age. Wife: Magdalena; children: Bernhard, heirs of son Adam, William, Anthony, Philip, Henry, Easie(?)(daughter), Elizabeth; grandchild: Margaret MCGRAW, "grandchild of my daughter Sarah"; executor: Nicholas GINTER; witnesses: Anthony GINTER, John AULABAUGH; written: 5 Mar 1817; probate: 26 Oct 1820; recorded: pg 136

KLINE, William - Mt Pleasant Twp. Wife: Catharina; children: Joseph, John, Andrew, Elizabeth wife of John PECHER, Mary, Catharina wife of Jacob STAUB, Susan, Abilona, Anna; executors: wife, Joseph HILT Sr.; witnesses: John WINTERODE, John SHORB; written: 18 Jan 1822; probate: 2 Feb 1822; wife renounced; recorded: pg 210

KNIGHT, John Conrad - Hamilton Twp. To be buried in Abbottstown Presbyterian meeting house year; daughter: Catharine WOLF; executor: daughter; witnesses: James WOLF, Tobias KEPNER; written: 20 Sep 1821; probate: 29 Jan 1823; recorded: pg 290

KNOUSE, Francis - Gettysburg. Children: Daniel, Hannah wife of Michael CONSER, Catharina, Eve wife of George CONSER, Elisabeth wife of Daniel KNOUSE, Sarah, Francis, George, Barbara wife of John ARENDT; executors: son-in-law John ARENDT, Christian WAMPLER; witnesses: Thomas MCKALIP, Henry HOKE; written: 31 Dec 1814; probate: 1 Oct 1819; recorded: pg 100

KNOX, George - Straban Twp. Wife: Elizabeth; children: Catharine wife of John STALLSMITH, Elizabeth wife of Peter SPANGLER, Peter; grandsons: George and John SPANGLER of Mary (deceased); Abraham SPANGLER to hold money in trust for grandsons; executors: Peter SPANGLER, David HARMAN; witnesses: George and Henry HOSSLER; written: 11 Apr 1823; probate: 29 Sep 1825; recorded: pg 428

KNOX, Mary - Hamiltonban Twp., widow. Children: Dr. Samuel, Margaret wife of Thomas COCHRAN; grandchildren: Mary COCHRAN, Elenor COCHRAN wife of William MCKNIGHT, John COCHRAN; executor: John ROBESON; witnesses: Walter SMITH, John GALLOWAY, Alexander RUSSELL; written: 13 Nov 1810; probate: 12 Aug 1818; recorded: pg 49

KNOX, Samuel - Adams Co., physician, weak. Wife: Rebeccah; children: John, Margaret wife of James MORROW (to receive Negro William GROCE), Samuel; executors: son Samuel, son-in-law James MORROW; witnesses: Walter SMITH, John MCCONAUGH, James MCNEELY; written: 1818; codicil: 20 Jun 1821; probate: 27 Dec 1821; recorded: pg 205

KRIDER, Jacob - town of Berlin. Wife: Eve; children: John, Jacob, Eve, Henry, Mary, Bastian; executors: wife, Andrew BRUNNER; witnesses: Henry PICKING, William PATTERSON; written: 22 Apr 1815; probate: 23 Sep 1817; BRUNNER, Baltimore city, renounced; recorded: pg 7

KUHN, Jacob - Mt Pleasant Twp., weak. Wife: Magdalena; children: Kitty, Terrease, Eve, Peggy, Mary, John, Joseph, Polly, Peter, Betsey; executors:

47

WILL BOOK C

John FOLLER, Peter BREECHNER; witnesses: John SHORB, Joseph RIDER, George HILL; written: 11 Mar 1825; probate: 7 Apr 1825; recorded: pg 400
    KUHN, Joseph - Hamilton Twp., sick. Wife: Catharine; children: Polly, Elizabeth, John, Emmanual/Samuel; executors: wife, Godleip BRIECHNER; witnesses: John BOWMAN, George BROWN; written: 13 Jan 1821; codicil: 2 Feb 1821; probate: 7 May 1821; recorded: pg 164
    KUHN, Joseph - Mt Pleasant Twp. Burial in Roman Catholic burial ground at Conewago Church; wife: Margaret; children: Elizabeth wife of Joseph MILLER, Margaret wife of Richard RICKROAD of Westmoreland Co., Pa., John; executor: son John, nephew Jacob KUHN; witnesses: David EDIE, William S. COBEAN, Michael GALLAGHER; written: 8 Sep 1823; probate: 20 Feb 1824; recorded: pg 352
    KUNTZ, George - Germany Twp., middling health. Wife: mentioned; children: Henry, Frederick, John (if living), Abraham, Andrew, Mary wife of George WELK, Susanna, Elizabeth wife of John Jacob WINTERODE, Catharine wife of Thomas LEMMON; executors: sons Henry, Frederick; witnesses: William SLYDER, Joseph LEFEVER Sr., Conrad PARR, Michael SHOLL Jr.; written: 9 Jun 1818; codicil: 29 Jul 1819; probate: 28 Apr 1823; recorded: pg 300
    LAWRENTZ, George - town of Berlin, unwell. Wife: Rebecca Bequest to children of counsin Nicholas KUHNOTT, Baltimore city; executors: wife, William JENKINS; witnesses: Frederick ASPER, William PATTERSON; written: 26 Feb 1818; probate: 2 Jul 1821; recorded: pg 190
    LEASE, Rebeckah - Menallen Twp., weak. Brothers: John, Mosses, David, Stephen, Joseph, George; executor: brother Mosses; witnesses: George WILSON, Samual RIGHT; written: 10 Feb 1819; probate: 10 Apr 1819; recorded: pg 90
    LEEPER, Eliza - Hampshire Co., Va., weak. Sisters: Martha WALTER, Eleanor SWENEY, Rebecca STEWART; executor: Isaac SWENEY, Adams Co.; witnesses: Thomas WALKER, John WALLIS; written: 10 Oct 1823; probate: 15 Dec 1823 in Va.,; recorded: pg 346
    LOBACH, Andrew - Latimore Twp., yeoman. Wife: Eve; children: Joseph, John, Peter, Samuel, Abraham, Polly, Elizabeth wife of Alexander ---, other daughters; executors: sons Abraham, Peter; witnesses: Jacob ALBERT, Jacob ERB Jr.; written: 22 Jul 1818; probate: 1 Aug 1818; recorded: pg 43
    LONG, Jacob - Conewago Twp., sick. Wife: Abigail; children: William, John, Catharina; mentions house in COlumbia, Lancaster CO., Pa.; executor: John HAUCK; witnesses: Jacob LONG, Christian FORNEY; written: 3 Mar 1820; probate: 21 Mar 1820; recorded: pg 120
    LONG, Jennet - Reading Twp., weak. Sons: William, Alexander; daughter-in-law Anny LONG; granddaughters: Nancy and Anny WALKER; wench Julianna to be sold; executors: son William, William PATTERSON; witnesses; Jacob KOHLER, Job DICKS; written: 4 Sep 1824; probate: 26 Apr 1825; recorded: pg 409
    LOWDEN, William - Liberty Twp., weak. Children: Samuel, Anny, Martha, William, Jane, Polly wife of James ROBERTS; executors and witnesses: David EICKER, Alexander MARCK; add'l witness: Joseph MAGINLY; written: 11 Mar 1822; probate: 20 Mar 1824; recorded: pg 359
    LOWMAN, John - Adams Co., weak. Sister: Mary CLARK; bequest to late brother-in-law John ZIMMERMAN; nephews and nieces: John, Sally, Charlotte LOVE, Peter KELLENBERGER; executors: John MARTIN, Thomas MCKEE; witnesses: Christian and Emanuel OVERHOLSER; written: 19 Apr 1822; probate: 2 May 1822; recorded: pg 219
    MARKS, Nicholas - Franklin Twp. Children: Peter, John, Daniel, Catherine wife of Peter MORETZ, Magdelena wife of Jacob MYERS, Barbara wife of Jacob MUNDORFF, Eve wife of Jacob WERTZ; daughter-in-law: Margaret wife of John;

WILL BOOK C

executor: son Peter; witnesses: Christian CULP, Robert WILLSON, Alexander RUSSELL; written: 25 Dec 1822; probate: 13 Dec 1823; recorded: pg 343

MARSDEN, James - Tyrone Twp., sick. Wife: Rachel; children: Eliza, John H., Leonard; executors: Thomas STEPHENS, John H. MARSDEN; witnesses: James L. NEELY, Edward HATTON; written: 7 Dec 1821; probate: 25 Dec 1821; recorded: pg 202

MARSDON, Mathew - Mt Pleasant Twp., advanced in age. Nephews and nieces: Phinas MARSDON of sister Peggy, Edward and Mathew WHITE, John and Leonard MARSDON; executors: nephew Phinas MARSDON, Edward WHITE; witnesses: Robert and John GILBRAITH, David NESBITT; written: 12 Jul 1822; probate: 6 Aug 1822; recorded: pg 247

MARSHALL, Peter Sr. - Oxford Twp., sick. Children: Margaret wife of Richard ADAMS (deceased), Elizabeth wife of Mathias MARTIN (deceased), Mary wife of Henry HEMLER, Anna wife of Joseph SHAFTER, Peter, heirs of Magdalena wife of Christopher WEIRICK, Catherine wife of John HEMLER; granddaughters: Catharine and Margaret of John (deceased); executors: son Peter, son-in-law Henry HEMLER; witnesses: Tobias KEPNER, Eleanor TIMMINS; written: 13 Feb 1819; probate: 23 Apr 1819; recorded: pg 93

MARTIN, Jesse - Menallen Twp., weak. Wife: Anny; brother John's children: Ann, Mary, Benjamin, John and Samuel; Jesse (FLEMING?), son of sister Sarah; Jesse BLOCH--- (page torn), son of sister Mary; executors: wife, Samuel WRIGHT son of Benjamin; witnesses: George, William B., Benjamin F. WILSON; written: 10 Mar 1817(?); probate: 24 Jan 1820; WRIGHT renounced; recorded: pg 93

MCCLAIN, James Sr. - Mt Pleasant Twp., sick. Wife: Elisabeth; children: John, James, Peter, Rachel widow of David WALSH, Catherine wife of John MUSSER, Elisabeth wife of Adam MARSHALL, Polly; two unnamed granddaughters of Peggy; executors: son James, Jacob WILL; witnesses: Samuel LILLY, Jacob METSGER; written: 20 Dec 1824; probate: 1 Feb 1825; recorded: pg 390

MCCONAUGHY, jane - Franklin Twp. Daughter: Susannah wife of Joseph WILLSON; grandchildren: Jinny, Susannah, Catharine, James King, Marthew Emelia WILLSON; executors: James KING, James HORNER; witnesses: Alexander and James M. HORNER; written: 11 Jun 1817; James HORNER renounced; probate: 2 May 1822; recorded: pg 222

MCCURDY, John - Straban Twp., weak. Mother: Agnes MCCURDY; wife: Catharina; daughters: Nancy, Elizabeth; executors: Jacob MYERS Sr., Valentine FICKES; witnesses: John BROUGH, Andrew WALKER; written: 6 Feb(?) 1818; probate: 12 Mar 1818; recorded: pg 26

MCELWEE, David - Cumberland Twp., weak. Bequests to: William L. NALLON, State of Jersey, sister's son; John and Jean WILLIAMSON, children of half brother; children of William HAMILTON; executor: William HAMILTON; witnesses: John EDIE, William SHEKLEY, Jesse HAMILTON; written: 13 Feb 1816; codicil: 18 Aug 1819; probate: 26 Feb 1821; recorded: pg 158

MCILVAIN, Andrew - Hamilton Twp. Children: Robert, Andrew, Mary, Margaret, Margery, Lolitia wife of James CUNNINGHAM, William; executors: sons William, Robert, Andrew; witnesses: Daniel GROSSERT, John L. GUBERNATOR; written: 9 Jul 1820; probate: 14 Nov 1820; recorded: pg 141

MCKEAN, Nancy - Liberty Twp., very sick. Bequests to: niece Nancy CALDWELL, daughter of Stephen CALDWELL; Emy Jane, eldest daughter of Samuel HUTCHESON; Christina daughter of William CALDWELL; Margaret daughter of John MYERS; unnamed brothers and sisters; executor: James WILSON; witnesses: John ARMSTRONG, William CALDWELL; written: 20 Jan 1819; probate: 12 Feb 1819; recorded: pg 66

WILL BOOK C

MCKINLEY, James - Liberty Twp., sick. Wife: Martha; children: James, John, Sarah, Rachel, Eliza, Peggy, Benjamin, William; executors: Alexander RUSSELL, James CUNNINGHAM; witnesses: Robert GRIER, Robert CUNNINGHAM; written: 6 Apr 1815; probate: 10 Feb 1823; recorded: pg 294

MCKINLEY, Martha - Adams County, weak. Children: Benjamin, William (not healthy); two unnamed sisters; executor: Thomas REID; witnesses: John C. BIGHAM, Mary Ann SLIDER; written: 14 Sep 1823; probate: 21 Oct 1823; recorded: pg 328

MCNAIR, Margaret - Liberty Twp., infirm. Children: Samuel, Nancy, Margaret BIGHAM, Isabella STEVENSON; grandchildren: Margaret daughter of Samuel, Margaret, Nancy and Alexander BIGHAM of Margaret; executor: daughter Nancy; witnesses: Francis KELLY, John MCELNEY; written: 29 Aug 1817; probate: 31 Oct 1817; recorded: pg 10

MCPEAK, Sarah - Liberty Twp. Niece: Margaret HASEL(?) wife of William; nephew: William MCPEAK; deceased father: Daniel MCPEAK; executors: George KERR, William MCPEAK; witnesses: George IRWIN, Jacob ROSSERMAN, J. SWENEY; written: 11 Sep 1819; probate: 14 Jan 1822; recorded: pg 208

MCSHERRY, Barnabas Sr. - Liberty Twp., weak. Housekeeper: Elizabeth WOLVERTON; nephews: Barnabas, Fredrick MCSHERRY; niece: Letitia GRAY; children of William MCSHERRY; executors: nephews: Barnabas, Fredrick MCSHERRY; witnesses: James CUNNINGHAM, Catherine BIGHAM; written: 15 Nov 1823; probate: 2 Mar 1824; recorded: pg 355

MELLINGER, David - Conewago Twp., sick. Wife: Ann Elizabeth; son: David, with wife and Abraham KEAGY to be guardians; executors: John HOSTETTER, John AULABAUGH; witnesses: Nicholas GINTER, John KREIGHTON; written: 24 Oct 1821; probate: 24 Nov 1821; recorded: pg 194

MERIDITH, Francis - Hamiltonban Twp., lastly a farmer. Son: Thomas; grandchildren: Francis and Jane MERIDITH wife of Joseph HILL; executor: Samuel WITHEROW; witnesses: John NICKLY, John ROBINSON, A. MAGINLY; written: 2 May 1820; probate: 14 Nov 1820; recorded: pg 143

MICHLE, Samuel - Straban Twp., weak. Children: Griffith, John, Thomas, Samuel, Robert, Jean, Sarah, Eve, Mary wife of Victor KING; executors: William GILLILAND Sr., Finley MCG---; witnesses: William WALKER, William GILLILAND Jr.; written: 23 Nov 1818; probate: 10 Apr 1819; recorded: pg 115

MIERS, Nicholas - Reading Twp. Children of first wife: Peggy wife of Jacob CRISWELL, John, Henry, Joseph, Susana, Sally, Samuel, WIlliam, David, Philip: wife: Mary; children: Peter, Catty, Abraham, Jacob, Solomon, George, Andrew, Michael, Jesse; land in Augusta Co., Va.; executors: William PATTERSON, Andrew BROUGH; witnesses: John NOGLE, James PATTERSON; written: 30 May 1820; probate: 22 Oct 1821; recorded: pg 329

MILLER, John - Conewago Twp., yeoman, very sick. Wife: Catharine; sister: Peggy wife of Peter NOEL; executors: wife, Peter SHAINFELTER; witnesses: Andrew MEHLHORN, John AULABAUGH; written: 2 Apr 1815; probate: 12 Mar 1821; recorded: pg 160

MILLER, Philip - Huntington Twp., weak. Wife: Rosanna; children: Gideon, Derrick, Jonathan, Charles, Lydia wife of Thomas CANNAN, Sarah wife of John MILLER, Rachel wife of Daniel MEALS, Elizabeth wife of Jacob PEISEL; grandchildren: Anne Sophia and Rachel PEISEL; executor: son-in-law Daniel MEALS; witnesses: Daniel SHEFFER, Charles MILLER; written: 30 Aug 1822; probate: 9 Sep 1822; recorded: pg 269

MISELEY, William - Huntington Twp., weak. Sister: Mary THOMPSON, if living; brother: John, if living; Elizabeth and Martha PEARSON; nephews and nieces: Elias PEARSON son of Isaac (deceased), Isaac PEARSON, Martha GARRETSON, Mary PEARSON, Ann PEARSON of Isaac, Everett, Lydia, Eliza and

WILL BOOK C

Thomas PEARSON of Thomas (deceased); executors: Joseph GRIEST Jr., Joel GARRETSON; witnesses: William WIERMAN, Uriah GRIEST; written: 22 Apr 1818; probate: 20 Jun 1818; recorded: pg 39
       MONTFORT, Peter - Mt Joy Twp. Daughter: Margaret DEITS; grandchildren: Peter HULICK, Peter Montfort DEITS, Henry, John and Abraham DEITS of New York State, Magdalena wife of Cornelius LOTT, Betsy COSHUN, Letty, Hannah, Mariah, Elizabeth Ann DEITS; executors: grandson Peter HULICK, Peter MONTFORT Jr.; witnesses: Jacob CASSAT, Jacob CASSAT Jr., John HAGERMAN; written: 25 May 1825; probate: 16 Aug 1825; recorded: pg 421
       MOOSE, Catharine - Franklin Twp., sick. Nephew: Jacob MOOSE; sister: Betsey MOOSE; executor: sister; witnesses: James KING, David WILLS; written: 30 Sep 1825; probate: 8 Nov 1825; recorded: pg 435
       MOWRER, John - Menallen Twp. Wife: Elizabeth; children: John, Barbara wife of Henry PETER, Peggy; granddaughters: Peggy and Hannah WALTER, Catharine WIDNER; executor: son John; witnesses: Philip LONG, George HARTZEL, Andrew WRAY; written: 7 May 1821; probate: 29 May 1821; recorded: pg 171
       MYERS, John - Hamiltonban Twp., weak. Wife: Cathrina; colored servant: Washington; children: Henry, Betsy, John, Rachel, Polly wife of Martin EBERT, Rebecca wife of Jacob KINER, Cathrine wife of George ZOLINGER; mentions six children of son Jacob; executor: son Henry; witnesses: James REID, John MARSHALL; written: 13 Apr 1821; probate: 28 May 1821; recorded: pg 168
       NOLL, John - Berwick Twp., very sick. Wife: Nancy; children: George, Joseph, others; executors: brother George NOLL, Tobias KEPNER; witnesses: Francis MARSHALL, John KRIM; written: 23 Mar 1817; probate: 29 Apr 1817; recorded: pg 1
       NORBECK, John - Mt Pleasant Twp., weak. To be buried in Roman Catholic burial ground at Conewago Church; wife: Rosina; children: mentioned; executors: wife, George LAWRENCE; witnesses: Peter LITTLE, John L. GUBERNATOR; written: 2 Nov 1824; probate: 26 Jan 1826; recorded: pg 440
       OVERHOLTZER, Christian - Liberty Twp., old. Wife: Christina; children: CHristian, Emanuel, Mary (eldest daughter), Christina (youngest); executor: James WILSON; witnesses: John ZIMMERMAN, John LOWMAN; written: 11 Feb 1819; probate: 22 Feb 1819; recorded: pg 70
       PIPER, Peter - Franklin Twp. Wife: Julianna; children: George, others; granddaughter: Polly REINHARD; executors: Jacob MUNDORFF, Jacob BEASACKER; witnesses: Jacob HILBERT, Jacob WEIDNER, John ARENDT; written: 15 Oct 1816; Jacob MUNDORFF renounced due to old age and being hard of hearing; probate: 7 Feb 1823; recorded: pg 291
       POFF(?), Christian - Adams County, weak. Wife: Elizabeth; children: John, Mary, Elizabeth and Mary (crossed out); executors: wife, son John; witnesses: William PATTERSON, Jacob WAYBRIGHT, Jacob FUNDERLIN; written: 12 Feb 1818; probate: 2 Mar 1818; recorded: pg 22
       REINECKER, George - McSherrystown, weak. Wife: Catharine; children: Catharine, Mary, Elizabeth, Susanah, Jacob (deceased), Leonard; grandson: George REINECKER; bequests made to daughters Elizabeth and Susanah as long as they didn't cohabit with their husbands John OBOLD and George OBERBAUGH; executors: Daniel EYSTER, Nicholas GINTER; witnesses: David MELLINGER, John KREIGHTON; written: 22 May 1820; EYSTER renounced; probate: 7 Aug 1822; recorded: pg 249
       REYNOLDS, John - Adams County, weak. Wife: Sophia; children: Mary wife of Bernard E. MURPHY, Margaret wife of John COTS, Elizabeth Ann wife of Joseph C. SHULTZ, John, Eleanor, Hugh; executor: son-in-law Joseph SHULTZ; witnesses: Henry WORTZ, Nathaniel GRASON, Samuel FLAGEL; written: 17 Jul 1825; probate: 22 Aug 1825; recorded: pg 423

WILL BOOK C

RHEA, Robert - Hamiltonban Twp., weak. Wife: Eliza; children: Crawford, John, James, Julian, Nancy, Polly; executors: son Crawford, Andrew MARSHALL; witnesses: John MARSHALL, Samuel BLYTHE, Joseph MCGINLY; written: 1 Jan 1825; probate: 24 Feb 1825; recorded: pg 396

RICHESON, Pheby - Hamilton Twp., widow, sick. Daughters: Teasy RICHESON, Jane wife of Michael RUPERTON; executor: Christian PICKING; witnesses: Peter DELLON, George BROWN; written: 10 Apr 1824; probate: 12 Jul 1824; recorded: pg 372

RIFE, Christian - Gettysburg, weak. Wife: Gertraut; children: Elizabeth wife of Nicholas SHEELY, Mary, Catharine wife of Andrew FORNEY; grandsons: John and Jacob SHEELY; executors: Nicholas SHEELY, Jacob EYSTER; witnesses: Christian CHRIETZMAN, Henry HOKE; written: 18 Aug 1818; probate: 28 Feb 1820; recorded: pg 110

RIFE, Henry - Menallen Twp. Wife: Barbara; children: Henry, Daniel, Jacob, Elizabeth wife of Peter CULP, Catherine wife of Jacob EICHOLTZ, Sarah wife of William GALBREATH, Barbara, Hannah; grandchildren: Eliza, Catharine, Susanna of Jacob; executors: sons Henry, Daniel; witnesses: Isaac WIERMAN, Stephen LEAS, John ARENDT; written: 21 Mar 18--; probate: 9 May 1820; recorded: pg 128

RIFE, Mary - Gettysburg, widow of Christian RIFE. Children: Mary, Catherine and Elizabeth SHEELY; executor: daughter Mary; witnesses: Christian CHRITZMAN, Henry HOKE; written: 21 Mar 1823; probate: 15 Mar 1824; recorded: pg 357

RISK, William - Menallen Twp., weak. Bequests to: Uriah, William, John, George children of William MOORE; William and Margaret MCGUNN(?), children of Margaret MCGUNN; William son of George WILSON; grandchildren of brother James RISK; children of sister Jane; wife: mentioned; executors: George WILSON, John EBERT; witnesses: Jacob and Eli THOMAS, John WRIGHT; written: 18 Jan 1818; probate: 29 Jan 1818; EBEWRT renounced; recorded: pg 15 (Note: surname is RUSK in renounciation and in 1810 census)

ROPE, Peter - Hamiltonban Twp., laborer, sick. Sisters: Catharine ROPE alias WILLIAMS, Susz BRONL(?); executor: Anthony SANDERS; witnesses: David WILSON Jr., William SHORT; written: 30 Aug 1821; probate: 22 Sep 1821; recorded: pg 176

ROUDEBUSH, Jacob - Menallen Twp. Wife: Elizabeth, also executor; witnesses: John and George HARTZELL, Andrew WRAY, Moses JENKINS; written: 13 Mar 1821; probate: 7 May 1821; recorded: pg 166

SAMPLE, John - Straban Twp. Wife: Jane; children: Jane wife of William ROSS, Sally, Polly, Peggy, James, John; executors: sons James and John, Robert MCMURDIS; witnesses: Walter SMITH, Alexander COBEAN; written: 15 Apr 1815; codicil: 27 Jun 1818 stating Polly now married, witnessed by William KING, Adam LIVINSTON Jr.; probate: 22 Oct 8121; recorded: pg 184

SANDERS, Jacob - Hamiltonban Twp., yeoman, weak. Wife: Christina; children: Abalone, Henry, Jacob; executor: John BLOCHER, weaver; witnesses: David WILSON Jr., Daniel BUTT; written: 26 Jul 1822; probate: 20 Dec 1822; recorded: pg 286

SAX, Sarah - Huntington Twp. Siblings: Jonathan and Benjamin BOWER, Rebecca wife of Michael MYERS; nieces: Rachel, Sarah, Mary MYERS; bequests to: Joseph ROSS son of Rebecca daughter of sister Rebecca; Elizabeth MCELWEE, Rachel wife of Frederick MYERS, Abraham and Benjamin ASPER; executor: brother Benjamin BOWER; witnesses: Daniel SHEFFER, Jonas YETTS; written: 26 Jun 1824; codicil: 1 Jul 1824; probate: 30 Apr 1825; BOWER renounced; recorded: pg 411

SAYER, Michael - Mt Joy Twp. Wife: Mary; only daughter: Elizabeth STONER separated by mutual agreement from John STONER; granddaughter: Eliza STONER;

52

WILL BOOK C

executor: Jacob MAYRING; witnesses: Philip HEAGY, William MCADAMS, Alexander RUSSELL; written: 1 May 1825; probate: 14 Dec 1825; recorded: pg 438
    SELL, Jacob - Germany Twp., weak. Wife: Christina; children: John, Eve wife of Jacob KEEFABER, Abraham, Henry, Jacob, Daniel, David, unnamed daughter wife of John UNGER, Peter; executor: son Jacob; witnesses: John SHILT, John KUGLER; written: 4 Feb 1816; probate: 7 Nov 1825; recorded: pg 433
    SHANNON, Alexander - Liberty Twp., weak. Wife: Isabela, also executor: witnesses: Thomas and Edward CATARINS, John DOUGHERTY; written: 4 Jan 1819; probate: 6 Nov 1819; recorded: pg 103
    SHECKLY, Margaret - Franklin Twp., sick. Widow(?) of George SHECKLY; children: William, Robert, Mary wife of William LARIMORE(?), Margaret wife of John HAMILTON, Nancy; grandchildren: Eliza Ann, George, Thomas SHECKLY; executors: sons William, Robert; witnesses; John GARVER, Robert FLETCHER; written: 12 Apr 1826; probate: 13 Oct 1825; recorded: pg 431
    SHEELY, Nicholas - Adams County, sick. Also SHEALLY. Wife: Elizabeth; children: Jacob, John, Mary, Barbara, Hannah, Elizabeth (deceased) wife of John WENTZ; executors: sons Jacob, John; witnesses: James RENSHAW, Detrich BISHOP, Peter and John SHEELY; written: 29 May 1823; probate: 12 Aug 1823; recorded: pg 313
    SHERER, Valentine - Germany Twp., weak. Wife: Mary; children: Ludwick, Andrew, George, Magdalen SNEER, Catharine HELM, Mary RIDDLEMOSER, Elizabeth wife of Abraham DIFFENDAL; bequest to children of Mary by Samuel DIFFENDAL (deceased); executors: son Ludwick, Christian LENTZ; witnesses: Robert MCILHINNY, Adam MILLER; written: 23 Feb 1813; probate: 22 Jan 1819; recorded: pg 63
    SHERMAN, George - Germany Twp., sick. Daughter-in-law Susanna SHERMAN widow of Jacob; grandchildren: George and Elizabeth SHERMAN; Negro Bill to be freed; mulatto girl Nancy SWOYER to finish servitude; bequest to Catharine BLOSSER; executors: daughter-in-law, John WEIKERT; witnesses: John PARR, George DOTTERER; written: 16 Feb 1822; probate: 31 May 1822; recorded: pg 229
    SHETRON, Jacob - Straban Twp., advanced in age. Also SITTEROWN. Children: John, Caty wife of Daniel DEARDORF, William, Margaret, Elizabeth, Mary Magdalen, Berbery, Mary, Susanna, Lidiah; executors: James RAINGE, Daniel HARMAN; witnesses: John BECHER, John BRINKERHOOF; written: 27 Jul 1820; probate: 19 Feb 1823; recorded: pg 296
    SHILT, Henry Sr. - Germany Twp., farmer, weak. Wife: Magdalena; unnamed children; executors: son John, Baltzer HILBERT; witnesses: Robert MCILHINNY, John HILBERT, Philip WARNER; written: 17 Aug 1813; probate: 2 mar 1820; recorded: pg 113
    SHRIVER, Andrew - Conewago Twp. Wife: Magdalin; unnamed children except John (bequest to his first wife's children); executors: sons David, Henry, Samuel; witnesses: Robert MCILHENNY, Frederick SNIDER, Daniel SNYDER; written: 27 Mar 1820; probate: 26 Sep 1823; recorded: pg 324
    SKIDMORE, John - Michael SPANGLER came to Register of Wills stating he witnessed verbal will made 8 Dec 1822; SKIDMORE died 14 Dec 1822; SPANGLER wrote will as remembered; probate: 27 Dec 1822; recorded: pg 288
    SLEMMONS, Robert Sr. - Hamiltonban Twp., farmer. Children: Robert, Anie(?), Rachael, John, James, Sarah wife of John PAXTON, Elizabeth wife of John TAYLER, Rebecca wife of James BLYTHE; executors: son Robert, James BLYTHE; witnesses: Amos MAGINLY, Ezra BLYTHE, William MCMILLAN Jr.; written: 29 Oct 1822; probate: 10 Nov 1823; recorded: pg 338
    SMITH, Frederick - Germany Twp., weak. Wife: Elisabeth; children, including Frederick and daughter wife of Henry MILLER; executors: son

WILL BOOK C

Frederick, son-in-law John CUGLER; witnesses: Robert MCILHENNY, George WILL; written: 7 Sep 1817; probate: 27 Jan 1819; recorded: pg 61
    SPRENKLE, Daniel - Hamiltonban Twp., sick. Wife: Christena; children: William, Daniel, George, Elizabeth wife of John MAYER, Charles, Catharine wife of Jacob STOVER, Polly wife of Peter ROSS, Eve wife of Joseph FLOSE(?), Lenah wife of Henry BOWSER; grandchildren: Thomas DAVIES, Julyann LOGAN, Eli, Charles, Betty, Peggy of Charles by his first wife; bequest to Catharine KLAUSER wife of Peter GIDEON; executors: wife, George WELSH; witnesses: Jacob HAFLEIGH/HAFLAIGH, John WEAGLE/WEAKLEY; written: 20 Oct 1821; probate: 20 May 1822; recorded: pg 226
    SPRENKLE, Henry Sr. - Germany Twp., yeoman, old and weak. Wife: Mary; children: Henry Jr., Michael, George, Anna Mary wife of Christian FORNEY, Elisabeth wife of Daniel WUNDER, Peter (deceased), Margaret wife of Philip KEEFER, Catharine, Susanna wife of John FOX; executor: John L. HINKLE; witnesses: Andrew WERTZ, Henry BEAR; written: 27 Apr 1817; probate: 23 Oct 1823; recorded: pg 331
    SPRING, Lawrence - Reading Twp., unwell. Wife: Susanna; executors: wife, William PATTERSON; witnesses: David CHRONISTER, John LAYDON; written: 2 Aug 1823; probate: 24 Nov 1824; recorded: pg 386
    STEIN, George Sr. - Conewago Twp., sick. Wife: Catharine; children: George, John, Peter, Elizabeth wife of Nicholas DOLHAMMER; executors: wife, Jacob HELSIGER; witnesses: Peter STORM, John ERISMAN; written: 21 May 1817; probate: 7 Jan 1818; recorded: pg 28
    STEHLEH, Joseph - Adams County. Also STEALY. Children: unnamed except for David; bequest to Jesse HALL; executors: sons Joseph, James; witnesses: Ludwick MILLER, Martin HELLER; written: 21 Sep 1823; probate: 14 Oct 1823; recorded: pg 326
    STERNER, John - Franklin Twp., weak. Children: Andrew, Jacob, Joseph, Elizabeth SNYDER; sister-in-law Mary; executor: David NEWMAN; witnesses: Jacob OYLER, Jacob BITTINGER; written: 7 Aug 1825; probate: 1 Feb 1826; recorded: pg 442
    STEWART, Charles - Gettysburg, weak. To be buried by the side of parents with stone such as they have; bequest to John ARENDT Sr., Isaac WIREMAN, children of brother David including John, Eliza, Libby, unreadable female, Nancy, Catharine Ann; to Martha Maria STEWART wife of David HORNER Jr., Margaret STEWART wife of Thomas MCKNIGHT, Moses Jinkins and his daughters: Ann Maria, Fanny and Libby wife of Thomas STEWART; to Maria DICKSON ("raised by us"); to Mary NEELY; Negro boy to be sold; executors: Moses JINKINS, Thomas MCKNIGHT, John MCCONAUGHY; witnesses: Francis ALLISON, Thomas J. COOPER; written: 3 Jun 1822; probate: 10 Jun 1822; MCCONAUGHY renounced; recorded: pg 233
    STEWART, James - Hamiltonban Twp., weak. Wife: Elizabeth; children: Ebenezer, William, David, James, Andrew, Margaret wife of Armstrong CAMPBELL, Jane; mentions John STEWART; executor: Samuel WITHEROW; witnesses: Alexander DOBBIN, William S. COBEAN, Alexander RUSSELL; written: 20 Aug 1818; probate: 8 Mar 1819; recorded: pg 76
    STIGERS, Joseph D. - Berwick Twp., hatter, sick. Mother: Elizabeth STIGERS; executor: --- HICKLY; witnesses: John AULABAUGH, John LEONARD; written: 4 Jun 1817; probate: 29 Aug 1817; recorded: pg 4
    STONER, Frederick - Mt Joy Twp., old, infirm. Wife: Deborah; children: Jacob, Fronecah CORNEL, Elizabeth STOCKSLAGLE, Magdalen KEHR, John, Abraham, Ann, Deborah; Abraham's daughters: Deborah, Catharine; executors: son John, daughters Ann, Deborah; witnesses: Daniel WELK, Robert MCILHINNY, Andrew

WILL BOOK C

HORNER; written: 1 Jul 1819; probate: 20 Sep 1822; daughters renounced; recorded: pg 272

STORM, Margaret - Conewago Twp., widow. To be buried in the Roman Catholic burial ground at Conewago Church; bequest to Rev. Mathias LEKEU; children: James, Anthony, Margaret wife of Englehart SMALL, Susannah wife of Jacob WISE, Sabina wife of Adam LANG, Mary (deceased) wife of Paul DREHER; grandchildren: Mary Margaret, Joseph, John, Anthony DREHER; executors: son James, son-in-law Jacob WISE; witnesses: John STEIGERS, John L. GUBERNATOR; written: 12 Nov 1825; probate: 21 Feb 1826; recorded: pg 443

SWOPE, Adam - Conewago Twp. Children: Jonathan, Samuel, Ephraim, Sarah, Eliza, Catharine (married); land in Greenbriar Co., Va.; executors: sons Jonathan, Samuel, Ephraim; witnesses: George DUTTERA, Philip RAHN, --- RENSHAW; written: 27 Dec 1820; probate: 14 Feb 1821; recorded: pg 155

TAYLOR, Joseph - Menallen Twp. Wife: Jane; children: George, William, Robert, Mary widow of Samuel YOUNG, Joseph, John, James Douglass; executor: son George; witnesses: Walter SMITH, John SELL, Alexander RUSSELL; written: 7 May 1816; probate: 6 Mar 1822; recorded: pg 216

THORNBURGH, Phebe - Huntington Twp. Brothers: William, Nicholas WIERMAN; bequests to: Louisa ROSS, Sarah WIERMAN widow of brother Benjamin and her sons Mark and Mills; executors: Thomas WIERMAN son of Nicholas, James ROBINETTE; witnesses: John WIERMAN, Jacob GARDNER; written: 30 May 1820; probate: 22 Jun 1822; recorded: pg 237

TOOT, David - Straban Twp. Wife: Margaret; children: mentioned; executors: brother Henry TOOT, George SMYZER; witnesses: Jacob BUCHER, John BATTORFF; written: 3 Oct 1821; probate: 27 Nov 1821; recorded: pg 199

TORRENCE, William - Mt Pleasant Twp., sick. Wife: Ann; children: Jinny wife of John WATSON, Mary, Rebeckah wife of Alexander MCGAUGHY, Ann, Aaron, John; grandson: William WATSON; executors: sons Aaron, John; witnesses: James HORNER, Andrew JOHNSON, Alexander RUSSELL; written: 6 Feb 1807; probate: 1 Nov 1820; recorded: pg 138

WAGGONER, Ludwick - Mt Pleasant Twp., sick. Wife: Catharine; executor: Ludwick SHEELY; witnesses: James LOCKART, Joseph DEETRICK Jr.; written: 21 May 1824; probate: 16 Nov 1824; recorded: pg 381

WALKER, William - Tyrone Twp., sick. Children: James, Andrew, Sally SPENCER, Ann SWISHER, Margaret wife of David CAMPBELL (to have land in Ohio), William, Robert; James WALKER to be guardian of William, Andrew WALKER and Abraham KING to be guardians of Robert's children; grandchildren: William, John, Mary, Margaret of Robert, Sally RANKIN of Sally SPENCER; executors: William PATTERSON, Abraham KING; witnesses: Jacob DEARDORFF, G. ARMER, Jacob KING; written: 28 Jun 1822; probate: 25 Jul 1822; recorded: pg 241

WARNUCH, Margaret - Franklin Twp., weak. Bequests to William McClean FOSTER, son of John FOSTER (deceased); to the children of Mrs. Enoch HAMILTON by both her first and present husbands; executor: Enoch HAMILTON; witnesses: John EDIE, John and Robert HAMILTON; written: 13 Mar 1815; probate: 1 May 1818; recorded: pg 34

WAUGH, William - Carroll's Delight, weak. Wife: mentioned; children: John, James, Alexander McClure, Polly CUNNINGHAM (of Muskingham Co., Ohio), William Pitt, Betsy PEDEN, Jane, Margaret, Amelia; grandchildren: William of Alexander, John Waugh CUNNINGHAM of Polly, William PEDEN of Betsy; Negro Jack to son John; Negro John MARSHALL to son James; executors: sons John, James; witnesses: Daniel MCALLISTER, William JOHNSTON, Zephuniah HERBET; written: 27 Nov 1817; codicil: bequest to granddaughter Jane of Jane written 27 Mar 1819; probate: 27 Oct 1823; recorded: pg 333

WILL BOOK C

WAYBRIGHT, Michael - Liberty Twp. Children: Michael, Martin, Matthias, Jacob, Elizabeth wife of Nicholas ---; executors: sons Matthias, Jacob; witnesses: Henry HOKE, James GETTYS, Alexander RUSSELL; written: 29 Aug 1803; probate: 1 Feb 1819; recorded: pg 65

WEAKLY, James - Reading Twp., weak. Sister: Polly; niece: Nancy JONES; bequests to: James MORISON and son William, William JENNET; mentions Dr. J. B. ARNOLD as his father's executor; executor: James ROBINETTE; witnesses: Allen and George ROBINETTE; written: 21 Jan 1820; probate: 2 Oct 1822; recorded: pg 276

WEAVER, Samuel - Straban Twp. Wife: Catharine; children: mentioned; executors: wife, brother Jacob WEAVER; witnesses: John SHRIVER, William GILLILAND; written: 11 Oct 1820; probate: 17 Oct 1820; recorded: pg 113

WEEMS, John - Germany Twp. Daughter: Frances WEEMS; grandson: Franklin Weems LEAS; bequests to: Franklin Weems DINWIDIE, Franklin Weems BLACK son of James BLACK, Ann MCCREARY and her daughter Jane, John Weems BLACK; executor: John Weems BLACK; witnesses: Andrew LITTLE Sr. and Jr., John BAIN; written: 24 Jul 1822; probate: 3 Sep 1822; recorded: pg 265

WIDNER, Daniel - Menallen Twp. Wife: Mary; children: Catherine, Sally, Polly, Jacob, Jonas, Lazarus, Daniel; executors: sons Jacob, Jonas; witnesses: Henry PETERS, John BENDER, George WILSON; written: 11 Jun 1822; probate: 29 Jul 1825; son Jacob renounced and letters granted to son Lazarus; recorded: pg 418

WIKERT, George - Mt Pleasant Twp., weak. Wife: Mary; children: Peter, Henry, Andrew, Peggy, Sally, and married daughters; bequests to: Polly COLESTOCK, Polly LIGHTNER, David COLESTOCK; executors: John WIKERT, James MCSHERRY; witnesses: Peter WIKERT, Philip RAHN; written: 7 Jul 1823; probate: 26 Jul 1823; recorded: pg 309

WILLIAMS, Jane - Menallen Twp. Son: John ADAMS and wife Mary; granddaughters: Eliza Jane and Maria Ann ADAMS; executor: George GRUPE (also GROUP); witnesses: John THOMAS, George WILSON; written: 11 Apr 1825; probate: 22 Feb 1826; GROUP renounced; letters granted to Michael C. CLARKSON; recorded: pg 445

WILSON, Thomas - Straban Twp., single man, unwell. Siblings: Robert, Elizabeth, Nancy wife of James REA/RAY; nephews: John and James of Robert; bequest to Polly SCOTT daughter of David SCOTT; sister Elizabeth to receive black girl Peggy; executors: brother Robert, John BRINKERHOOF; witnesses: James KING, Garret BRINKERHOOF; written: 4 Sep 1817; probate: 10 Nov 1817; recorded: pg 11

WINTERODE, John Sr. - Petersburg (Littlestown), Germany Twp., weak. Wife: Catharine; children: Samuel, Henry, Mary wife of George WILL, Andrew; executors: son Andrew, son-in-law George WILL; witnesses: Robert MCILHINNY, Jacob RIDDLEMOSER, Michael DEISERT; written: 27 Aug 1821; signed WINROTT; probate: 9 Oct 1821; recorded: pg 178

WINTRODE, Jacob - Gettysburg, weak. Wife: Margaret; children: mentioned; deceased father-in-law Henry SLAGLE; executors: George NEAS, James MCSHERRY; witnesses: Alexander SPEER, William HOSTETTER; written: 16 Aug 1823; probate: 18 Sep 1823; recorded: pg 321

WOLF, Philip Sr. - Germany Twp., sick. Wife: Magdalena; children: mentioned; executors: sons John, Philip, John BOWER; witnesses: Robert MCILHINNY, Joseph HENRY; written: 26 Nov 1821; probate: 6 Feb 1822; recorded: pg 213

WOLFORD, Peter - Mt Pleasant Twp., sick. Wife: Barbara; children: George, Peter; executors: wife, Henry BRINKERHOFF; witnesses: Peter and Joseph SMITH; written: 2 Jun 1818; probate: 7 Jun 1818; recorded: pg 42

WILL BOOK C

WRIGHT, John - Menallen Twp., weak. Wife: Elizabeth; children: Mary, Debborah wife of Jonathan POTT(?), Elizabeth wife of Jacob HACH(?), Ruth widow of Thomas(?) HAMMOND, Sarah wife of George WILSON, John, William, Nathan; executors: son William, son-in-law George WILSON; witnesses: Christian, John and Jacob BENDER; written: 15 Aug 1817; probate: 4 Jul 1820; recorded: pg 131

ZETTLE, William - Franklin Twp., sick. Wife: Mary; children: Conrad, Mary, Margaret, Elizabeth; executors: Peter MICKLEY, John ARNDT; witnesses: Henry HOKE, Joseph PITZER; written: 10 Mar 1820; probate: 22 Feb 1820; recorded: pg 108 (Note: dates as recorded)

INDEX

?nobarger - 29
?rine - 33
Acker - 10
Ackerman - 16
Adair - 1,8,13,16,44,46
Adams - 8,10,12,13,14,16,22,23,
    25,27,38,49,56
Agnew - 6,8,11,15,16,38,41,42
Akerman - 16
Albert - 22,33,38,48
Algist - 22
Alison - 34
Allen - 2,39
Allison - 54
Altemas - 1
Annan - 46
Apley - 38
Arendt - 23,33,35,47,51,52,54
Armer - 55
Armstrong - 29,34,36,37,49
Arndt - 1,13,57
Arnold - 11,14,15,19,26,34,35,
    38,40,56
Ashbaugh - 16,32,33
Asper - 1,10,30,33,38,48,52
Attig - 10,30,45
Aughinbaugh - 45
Aulabaugh - 20,22,29,32,34,46,
    47,50,54
Aulebaugh - 25,30,34
B-- - 46
Baer - 16
Bagher - 15
Bailey - 7,16
Baily - 30
Bain - 56
Baisore - 39
Baker - 1,9,21,31
Baldridge - 38
Bales - 10,35
Balmer - 14
Balsly - 17
Bankerd - 20
Bardt - 5,10,27,38
Bare - 5,23
Bargold - 34
Barr - 7,16,44,46
Barrett - 44
Barron - 9,11
Bart - 8,46
Bateman - 30
Battorff - 55
Baugher - 30
Baum - 22

Baumgardner - 34
Bayer - 4
Beaker - 38
Beals - 1,14,16,28
Bear - 16,32,38,45,54
Beard - 9,16,17
Beasacker - 38,51
Beaty - 20
Bechdol - 11
Becher - 1,11,29,53
Becker - 24
Beecher - 36
Beesacker - 18
Begen - 25
Behtel - 20
Beitler - 2
Bell - 19
Bellence - 3
Bender - 16,17,24,30,39,56,57
Bennedict - 12
Benner - 38
Bennett - 45
Bentz - 28
Bentzel - 45
Bercaw - 1,39,46
Bereand - 44
Berger - 14
Berninger - 17
Bertz - 4
Bettu - 38
Biehl - 14
Bier - 45
Bigham - 1,6,10,17,29,30,34,41,50
Billinger - 23
Binder - 1,10
Bingham - 31
Bishop - 53
Bittinger - 17,54
Black - 7,12,17,26,32,56
Blackburn - 24,30
Blaesser - 1,3,5,18,20,24
Blank - 20,21
Blankley - 11
Blankly - 45
Blear - 8
Bleckley - 18
Bleckly - 22
Blish - 40
Bliver - 17
Blocher - 38,52
Blosser - 45,53
Blyth - 4
Blythe - 1,6,19,21,25,52,53
Bogle - 2

INDEX

Boll-- - 5
Bonner - 12,18,22
Bosserman - 5,31
Bougle - 11
Bouser - 8
Bower - 1,11,17,22,30,31,35,38,
    39,52,56
Bowers - 39
Bowman - 31,48
Bowser - 5,54
Boyd - 9,23,28,39
Boyer - 4,27,35,37
Boyle - 46
Bracken - 4
Brackenridge - 39
Bradshaw - 44
Brady - 41
Brandon - 2,17,18
Branner - 18
Branon - 18
Branwood - 18
Bream - 45
Breckenridge - 32
Breden - 6,43
Breechner - 48
Breighner - 27
Brenison - 41
Brice - 1,11,12,19
Briechner - 48
Briegner - 22
Brilhart - 23
Brines - 13
Brineshold - 37
Bringman - 1
Brinkerhof - 2,18,37
Brinkerhoff - 3,20,33,39,43,56
Brinkerhoof - 33,40,53,56
Britan - 18
Britt - 39
Britzher - 46
Bronl - 52
Brosius - 3,11,15
Brothers - 23,26,27,46
Brough - 49,50
Brown - 1,2,5,7,8,18,20,23,25,
    26,27,31,40,46,48,52
Bruch - 29
Brunner - 47
Bryns - 3
Buchanan - 25
Bucher - 37,55
Bumbaugh - 1
Bumgardtner - 18
Bumgartner - 18

Burkholder - 18
Burns - 7
Buse - 18
Bush - 24
Bushey - 3,17
Bushman - 40,45
Bushy - 2,11,18
Butt - 52
Byer - 6
Byers - 13
Caldwell - 1,3,6,18,38,49
Calhon - 21
Calvin - 42
Camp - 46
Campbell - 1,2,4,19,35,40,54,55
Canan - 22
Cannan - 50
Carbaugh - 18
Carle - 19
Carnohan - 9
Carrick - 19
Carson - 9,14,24,28
Carvin - 45
Cashman - 2,7,33,40
Cassat - 2,16,19,40,51
Cassatt - 31
Catarins - 53
Cereshter - 23
Chamberlain - 19,30,40,41,45
Chamberlin - 40,41
Chambers - 25,36
Charles - 43
Chester - 6
Chrietzman - 52
Christ - 39
Chritzman - 52
Chronister - 32,54
Clark - 18,38,48
Clarkson - 56
Cleaver - 3
Clements - 29
Clerk - 11
Cline - 27,38
Clopper - 2
Clunk - 20
Cluts - 3,9,19
Clutz - 11
Coale - 29
Cobean - 3,4,5,9,12,13,18,19,22,23,
    24,28,34,41,42,43,48,52,54
Cobright - 12
Cochran - 3,11,12,27,28,47
Cole - 19,40
Colestock - 56

59

INDEX

Collins - 12,40
Colter - 19
Comisky - 41
Comly - 35
Commongore - 20
Conrad - 25,45
Conrod - 24
Conser - 47
Cook - 13,14,40,41
Cooper - 24,28,40,41,45,54
Coopser - 7
Coplin - 13
Copperstone - 11
Copponhafer - 32
Cornel - 54
Coshun - 41,51
Cots - 51
Coulogue - 25
Coulson - 14,22,44
Coulter - 7,25,35
Coutler - 40
Cover - 17,40
Cox - 2
Craighead - 35
Crawford - 21
Cress - 20
Crilly - 29
Crin - 24
Crissimere - 19
Criswell - 13,50
Croley - 41
Cronbaugh - 25
Cronister - 43
Crooks - 25
Cross - 3,17,19,39
Crowel - 33
Crownover - 39,41
Crum - 20,23,43
Crysher - 41
Cugler - 54
Culp - 20,32,49,52
Cummins - 16
Cunningham - 17,34,41,49,50,55
Cupser - 20
Dady - 7
Danner - 3,19
Darnell - 26
Daugherty - 41
Davies - 54
Davis - 28
Day - 6,38,41
Deal - 43
Deardoff - 41
Deardorf - 53

Deardorff - 24,41,55
Dearduff - 10
DeBarth - 27,29,34,39
Deck - 38
Decker - 20
Deel - 20
Deemer - 40
Deetrick - 55
Deffendal - 20
Degroff - 40
Degroft - 2
Degroftt - 36
Dehl - 27
Deisert - 2,56
Deitrick - 15
Deits - 51
Delap - 2,3,6,9,30,35,41,42
Dellon - 52
Dellone - 20,47
Demaree - 7,20,39
Demarer - 30
Demarest - 20
Detrick - 14,35
Detter - 39
Deveny - 17
Dever - 28
Devison - 1
Dewalt - 47
Dewolt - 9
Dich - 42
Dickey - 3
Dicks - 35,48
Dickson - 12,20,22,26,42,44,54
Diehl - 20,41
Diel - 42
Diffendal - 53
Digges - 8
Dill - 9,14,20,21,35,36
Dillon - 30
Dinwidie - 56
Dinwody - 30
Discon - 21
Ditterhefer - 40
Divin - 31
Dixon - 34,40
Dobbin - 4,6,16,19,21,28,42,43,54
Dobbins - 6
Dodds - 2
Dolhammer - 54
Donaldson - 9
Dorsough - 6
Dortitch - 3
Dotterer - 21,53
Dougherty - 3,53

60

INDEX

Douglass - 3,6,25,42
Downey - 21
Drak - 25
Dreher - 55
Driskell - 11
Duff - 28
Dull - 24
Dunwoddy - 3
Dunwoody - 17,21,30,36,42,44
Durborrow - 36
Duttera - 55
Eable - 2
Eakins - 40
Early - 24
Ebbert - 13
Ebert - 24,51,52
Eck - 20
Eckart - 29
Eckenrode - 21
Eckenroth - 12
Eckenrott - 33
Ecker - 38
Eckert - 36,43
Eckord - 36
Edie - 3,5,9,21,24,28,29,32,34,
    42,45,48,49,55
Ehrman - 3
Eichelberger - 19,46
Eicholtz - 29,52
Eicker - 48
Eighholtz - 21
Ekert - 21
Elbert - 32,42
Elden - 3
Eldendice - 30
Elder - 22
Eley - 9
Eliott - 36
Elliott - 14,43
Ellis - 43
Emmit - 44
Enk - 25
Epley - 43
Erb - 29,48
Erbach - 24
Eresman - 23
Erhart - 3
Erisman - 54
Ervin - 21
Erwin - 3
Espy - 36
Essick - 43
Essig - 33,43
Essom - 8

Ester - 15
Everitt - 3
Ewing - 3,13,21,22,27,28,37,45
Eyster - 14,18,20,43,46,51,52
Fahnestock - 25,29,30,31,34,47
Falex - 22
Falk - 2
Fanerstock - 17
Fanestock - 43,47
Feeser - 22
Feesse - 32
Fegen - 6
Felty - 22
Fence - 25
Fergus - 3
Ferguson - 4,17,25
Ferkes - 4
Fickes - 2,14,17,22,23,38,43,44,49
Fickle - 22
Fillen - 24
Findly - 46
Fink - 20,22,36,46
Finley - 4
Fisher - 30,43
Fiskes - 22
Fissel - 13,22
Fitter - 21
Flagel - 51
Flatcher - 9
Fleager - 5
Fleak - 22
Fleck - 4,5,11,22,35
Fleger - 5
Flemen - 30
Flemin - 11
Fleming - 22,26,49
Flesley - 20
Fletcher - 4,12,16,23,24,28,39,53
Fleur - 6
Flick - 14
Floar - 13
Flohr - 38,43
Flore - 39
Flori - 23
Flose - 54
Foal - 17
Foals - 23
Foller - 27,48
Forner - 1
Forney - 48,52,54
Forrey - 30
Forry - 43,47
Foster - 4,55
Foulk - 12

INDEX

Fox - 54
Frauss - 25
Frazier - 35
Freed - 23
Freise - 23
Fried - 15,43
Fundenburg - 47
Funderlin - 51
Funk - 16,41
Furgeson - 46
Furgus - 3
Gaisel - 4
Galbraith - 23
Galbreath - 29,52
Galicien - 30
Gallagher - 4,48
Gallaher - 23
Galloway - 3,38,42,46,47
Gamble - 6
Gardner - 22,43,55
Gareter - 36
Garner - 35
Garretson - 23,39,50,51
Garrett - 16
Garver - 53
Garvin - 26,43
Geiselman - 36
Gelvix - 4
Gelwicks - 30
Gettis - 36
Gettys - 8,18,23,32,56
Getz - 4
Ghesler - 24
Gibson - 24,34
Gice - 24
Gideon - 54
Giffen - 4,46
Gilbert - 4,23,33,44,45
Gilbraith - 49
Gilchrist - 23
Gilespy - 20
Gill - 31
Gilleland - 22,23,32,36
Gillenan - 6
Gilliland - 2,4,7,8,10,11,14,23
24,26,33,37,43,44,
45,50,56
Gillmyer - 44
Gimber - 25
Ginder - 5,13
Ginkins - 35
Ginter - 34,47,50,51
Ginther - 5,13
Gitt - 28,45

Glasgow - 8
Glass - 32
Gminder - 24
Gobricht - 27
Godfrey - 14,35,44
Golden - 23,41,42
Good - 29
Gorley - 4
Gossler - 1
Goudey - 24
Gourley - 5
Grable - 32
Gracely - 24
Graff - 14
Graft - 5,10,12,19,31
Graham - 8,10,24,44
Grason - 51
Gray - 6,42,44,50
Graybell - 5
Greenemyer - 13
Greenewald - 44
Greer - 3,44
Greglow - 45
Greist - 39
Grible - 39
Grichtin - 34
Grier - 9,39,50
Griest - 14,15,16,35,51
Griffith - 24,38
Grim - 8
Grist - 2,32,38
Groce - 47
Groft - 44
Groop - 10,30,45
Groover - 44
Groscort - 7
Groscost - 5,31
Groscrost - 6
Gross - 20,24
Grossert - 49
Group - 2,5,31,56
Grove - 5
Grupe - 10,56
Gubernator - 6,7,12,27,31,38,49,51,55
Gunkel - 35
Gunkle - 41
Gurlay - 5
Guynn - 45
Hach - 57
Hadden - 1
Haflaigh - 54
Hafleigh - 54
Hagen - 14
Hagerman - 51

62

INDEX

Hagst - 9
Hall - 5,6,17,24,43,54
Hamilton - 9,24,25,26,28,32,49,
    53,55
Hammond - 5,6,24,44,57
Handley - 20
Hanes - 28
Hanley - 8
Hansleman - 13
Harlan - 3
Harlen - 24
Harman - 47,53
Harper - 13
Harret - 44
Harris - 22,24,36
Harry - 18
Harshey - 28
Hart - 1,14,18,25
Hartman - 5,20,24,44
Hartzel - 12,45,51
Hartzell - 52
Hartziger - 7
Hasel - 50
Haspelhorn - 27
Hatten - 24
Hatton - 2,11,43,44,45,49
Hauck - 48
Hauptman - 9
Hayes - 16,24,28,38,42
Hays - 42
Heagen - 17
Heagey - 45
Heagy - 17,21,33,45,53
Heck - 45
Heckenluber - 45
Hefer - 17
Hegan - 17
Hegi - 8
Heikes - 25
Heim - 38
Hein - 16
Heiner - 32
Heller - 44,54
Helm - 53
Helsiger - 54
Hemler - 5,49
Hence - 7
Hendricks - 9,30,47
Henry - 17,56
Herbert - 21
Herbet - 55
Herman - 5,18,38,39
Hershey - 25,45
Herter - 20

Hess - 5
Hewitt - 6,9,14,17,30
Hickenluber - 11,33
Hickley - 15,34
Hickly - 54
Higas - 25
Hilberadt - 34
Hilbert - 27,51,53
Hildebrand - 16,29,30,32
Hill - 11,25,41,48,50
Hilldebrand - 16
Hillebush - 25
Hilt - 47
Himes - 24
Hinct - 38
Hinkle - 4,26,33,38,45,54
Hobaugh - 6
Hodge - 19,27,45
Hoffman - 6,17,22,25,44
Hofman - 23
Hoghtallen - 2
Hoke - 1,4,5,8,10,23,25,29,36,43,45,
    46,47,52,56,57
Hollinger - 5,10,15,25,27,45
Hollobaugh - 25
Holmes - 4
Hoofnagle - 46
Hoover - 8,16,29,35,36
Hoppert - 36
Horn - 2
Hornberger - 25, 43
Horner - 8,22,28,29,46,49,54,55
Hosack - 12
Hossler - 47
Hostetter - 19,36,50,56
Houck - 45
Houghtalen - 1
Houghtaling - 20
Housell - 43
Howel - 14,20
Howie - 1,6,9
Huet - 2
Huffman - 4
Huffnagle - 46
Hughs - 25
Hulick - 39,51
Hull - 2,8,15,46
Humphrey - 4
Hunt - 44
Hunter - 8,10,12,14,16,37,40,44,46
Husel - 17
Hushey - 32
Huston - 6,33
Hutcheson - 6,35,42,49

63

INDEX

Hutchison - 28,45
Hutton - 6,9,31,36
Irvin - 26
Irvine - 4
Irwin - 3,4,50
Jackson - 43
Jacobs - 1,38,45
Jameson - 10,20,30,31
Jardan - 18
Jenkins - 6,22,25,32,33,34,40,
    44,46,48,52
Jennet - 56
Jinkins - 28,54
John - 9,40
Johns - 18
Johnson - 55
Johnston - 2,4,8,14,28,55
Johnton - 35
Jones - 2,4,6,26,35,46,47,56
Jonston - 20,23
Joyce - 45
Judson - 6
Kaegy - 6
Kagey - 19
Keagy - 6,50
Kearney - 25,46
Keas - 26
Keckler - 18
Keefaber - 53
Keefer - 27,54
Keefhauver - 46
Keefhaver - 40,47
Keener - 45
Kefer - 46
Kehlenberger - 12
Kehr - 54
Kellenberger - 26,27,33,48
Kelly - 18,29,38,44,45,50
Ken - 8
Kenady - 45
Kendel - 40
Kenedy - 24
Keney - 31
Kenneday - 40
Kennedy - 14,24,40
Keplinger - 10,46
Kepner - 1,4,10,15,17,20,21,22,
    28,30,36,46,47,49,51
Kerbaugh - 6,8
Kern - 8
Kerr - 3,5,6,7,9,12,19,20,21,22,
    23,26,35,37,50
Kesler - 44
Kessler - 7

Killenberger - 12
Kimmel - 13,29,47
Kiner - 51
Kinerd - 16
Kinert - 18
King - 7,16,20,21,26,31,35,39,40,42,
    44,49,50,51,52,55,56
Kinyon - 40
Kissinger - 7
Kitch - 18
Kitchen - 8,39
Kitchon - 25
Kitsmiller - 33
Kittlewell - 38
Kitzmiller - 8,26,27,45,46,47
Klapsaddle - 33
Klauser - 54
Klein - 27
Kline - 25,47
Klunk - 3,38
Knight - 5,29,47
Knouff - 27
Knous - 38,42,43
Knouse - 47
Knox - 4,19,27,30,45,47
Koch - 3,5,27,36
Koenig - 23
Kohler - 29,48
Kohlstock - 2,7,27
Kolb - 7
Koons - 29
Kosser - 45
Kott - 29
Kraft - 7,27
Kraps - 26
Kreighton - 50,51
Kreiss - 7
Krider - 47
Krim - 51
Kugler - 53
Kuhn - 3,9,11,12,22,27,31,47,48
Kuhnott - 48
Kuhns - 10
Kunkle - 4
Kuns - 20
Kuntz - 7,9,10,22,27,48
Kupser - 7,20
Kyle - 21,35
Labaugh - 39
Laird - 8,12,32
Lampin - 19
Lang - 7,14,55
Lanver - 18
Larence - 22

INDEX

Larimore - 53
Lashell - 32
Lashells - 28,42
Latshaw - 18,31
Latta - 5
Laughlin - 12
Lauman - 7
Lawimer - 32
Lawrence - 51
Lawrentz - 48
Laydon - 54
Lear - 6
Leas - 27,33,52,56
Lease - 41,48
Leatherwood - 24
Leav - 6
Leckey - 7,13
Leece - 30
Leech - 14,16
Leeper - 48
Leese - 13
Lefever - 48
Lehman - 27
Leidner - 20
Leinert - 24
Leiser - 38
Leister - 36
Lekeu - 55
Lemmen - 4
Lemmon - 48
Lentz - 53
Leonard - 23,54
Levingston - 26
Levinston - 41
Light - 7
Lightenwallen - 14
Lightewalter - 11
Lightner - 14,26,56
Lilly - 3,8,11,22,27,34,38,39,
    41,49
Linah - 40
Linetuer - 6
Lingafelter - 8
Lingefelter - 4,31
Linn - 4,17,22
Little - 5,25,27,36,39,51,56
Livinston - 52
Lobach - 48
Lobache - 31
Lobaugh - 22
Lockart - 55
Lockhart - 22,27,37
Logan - 54
Lohr - 27

Lonenacher - 41
Long - 8,18,20,26,27,28,34,36,45,
    48,51
Longsiner - 20,23
Longwell - 14,42
Lorre - 25
Lorrimer - 28
Lott - 39,41,51
Lour - 25
Loure - 32
Love - 7
Low - 2
Lowden - 48
Lowman - 7,48,51
Lowrey - 26
Lowstetter - 30
Mack - 38
Magaffin - 19
Maginly - 1,6,17,21,48,50,53
Magoffin - 26
Magossen - 42
Mahn - 18
Mailhorn - 35
Major - 28
Males - 35
Maloney - 44
Manfort - 39
Marck - 48
Mark - 9,13,18,20,43
Marks - 13,29,48
Marsden - 49
Marsdon - 49
Marshall - 8,9,10,21,22,28,46,49,51,
    52,55
Martin - 1,2,4,9,16,25,29,48,49
Mather - 36
Matter - 19
Maxfield - 2
Maxwell - 26,28,32,35,36
May - 2,10
Maye - 32
Mayer - 54
Mayring - 53
Mc-- - 42
McAdams - 53
McAlister - 8
McAllen - 28
McAllister - 36,55
McCaffrey - 26
McCalmod - 36
McClain - 49
McClanahan - 39
McClean - 4,8,11,13
McCleary - 8,24,25,31,41

65

INDEX

McCleave - 6
McCleland - 3
McClellan - 5,8,17,21,25,28
McCley - 9
McClure - 24,29
McCollough - 32
McConaugh - 47
McConaughey - 40
McConaughy - 4,8,10,16,17,18,22,23, 24,26,28,34,42,49,54
McConomy - 9
McCracken - 35
McCraken - 9
McCrea - 11
McCreary - 4,13,17,35
McCullough - 16,26
McCurdy - 3,10,28,35,49
McDermant - 22
McDonald - 5
McDowel - 9
McEheney - 31
McElnay - 29,50
McElwain - 7,28
McElwane - 6
McElwee - 49,52
McFarland - 10
McFarlane - 41,42
McFindley - 14
McG-- - 50
McGarvey - 11
McGaughey - 10
McGaughy - 3,9,26,55
McGinley - 8,9,21,35
McGinly - 1,19,25,52
McGinty - 46
McGlaughlin - 9,40
McGonaughy - 41,42
McGraiel - 9
McGraw - 47
McGren - 31
McGrew - 2,3,5,7,9,14,18,23,24,25, 28,29,33,35,41,42,44
McGunn - 52
McIlhenney - 27
McIlhenny - 16,20,26,27,31,37,42, 53,54
McIlhiney - 20,26
McIlhinny - 1,7,8,10,12,15,16,22, 27,29,36,46,47,53,54,56
McIlnay - 19
McIlvain - 24,49
McIlwain - 38
McIntire - 7
McJensey - 19

McJimsey - 35
McKaleb - 26
McKalip - 47
McKean - 49
McKee - 7,9,21,48
McKelip - 24
McKesson - 11
McKilep - 16
McKinley - 1,10,50
McKinney - 17
McKnickle - 9
McKnight - 29,47,54
McKnitt - 42
McLaughlin - 29
McLean - 44
McMalen - 18
McMaster - 6
McMillan - 53
McMillen - 11,42
McMordie - 29
McMullan - 1
McMullen - 18,23
McMumm - 8
McMurdis - 52
McMurdy - 9
McMurray - 19
McNair - 11,46,50
McNeely - 47
McNutt - 12,25
McPeak - 50
McPherson - 4,6,9,21,22,25,29,34
McQuin - 9
McResson - 42
McSherry - 12,29,50,56
McVear - 29
Meals - 24,50
Mearing - 11
Meckly - 9
Mehlhorn - 50
Meichl - 24
Meil - 32
Melhorn - 4
Mellinger - 35,50,51
Melown - 7
Menchey - 7,44
Mentieth - 7
Meredith - 6,25
Meridith - 50
Meshler - 9
Messersmith - 9
Metsger - 49
Metzger - 8,23
Meyer - 1,13
Meyrs - 41

INDEX

Michael - 33
Michle - 50
Mickley - 19,38,43,57
Middlecoff - 40
Miers - 50
Miley - 14,29,30
Milhime - 31
Miller - 1,4,6,8,9,11,12,17,21,22,
    23,26,29,30,32,34,35,38,
    40,44,48,50,53,54
Minder - 17
Minich - 35
Minigh - 27
Miseley - 50
Missenhimer - 18
Mitchell - 2
Money - 6,9
Monfort - 2,14
Monshour - 29
Monshower - 31
Montfort - 51
Montorf - 13
Moor - 4
Moore - 5,6,8,9,10,13,17,30,40,
    44,52
Moorhead - 13,17,18
Moose - 51
Moretz - 48
Morgan - 14
Morison - 24,28,56
Moritz - 30
Morningstar - 7
Morrow - 5,28,30,32,34,45,47
Morton - 30
Mortorff - 33
Moser - 20
Mouse - 20,27
Mowrer - 51
Mullan - 1
Mummert - 1,31,34
Mumper - 18
Mundorff - 13,18,35,48,51
Muntorf - 33
Murphy - 22,51
Murrat - 10
Murret - 10
Mussear - 21
Musselman - 46
Musser - 49
Myer - 5,10,30,37
Myers - 10,16,18,22,25,27,28,30,
    32,38,41,43,48,49,51,52
Nace - 28,33

Nagle - 24,30
Nallon - 49
Naugle - 5
Neal - 39,45
Neas - 56
Neaswitz - 16
Neelle - 7
Neely - 6,10,11,14,22,30,31,33,49,54
Neesbit - 12
Neety - 2
Nell - 3
Nesbitt - 49
Newland - 30
Newlin - 14
Newman - 29,54
Nickel - 10,17,22,30,41,42
Nickle - 5
Noel - 22,29,30,50
Nogle - 50
Nolan - 25
Noll - 15,17,30,36,46,51
Norbeck - 51
Null - 19,25,45
O'Blenis - 10,30
Oberbaugh - 51
Obis - 10
Obold - 5,6,15,51
Obolt - 11
Occer - 6
Odle - 41
Oliver - 44
Ommerman - 3
Orr - 35,42
Overholser - 48
Overholtzer - 51
Owings - 30,46
Oyler - 1,11,54
Parker - 6
Parr - 10,20,48,53
Patterson - 1,3,7,9,10,11,14,18,19,
    25,30,31,35,36,40,41,43,
    45,47,48,50,51,54,55
Patton - 12,21
Paxton - 16,19,21,23,28,53
Pearsen - 31
Pearson - 2,3,6,14,23,24,35,50,51
Pecher - 19,30,38,40,47
Pedan - 11
Peden - 55
Peisel - 50
Pellentz - 3,11
Pence - 38
Penrose - 14,15

67

INDEX

Petenturph - 10
Peter - 51
Peters - 56
Peterson - 2
Pettit - 31
Pfoutz - 20,31,32
Philips - 19
Picking - 2,7,34,40,47,52
Pidgeon - 23
Pilkington - 4,31
Piper - 51
Pittendorf - 24
Pitzer - 57
Plank - 17,23
Plump - 45
Poff - 51
Pollock - 11,14,35
Polly - 33
Porsel - 38
Porter - 9,11,12,31
Pott - 57
Potter - 10
Pottorf - 18
Pounds - 36
Pressel - 1
Pressell - 31
Procter - 5,11
Proctor - 22
Puffenberger - 9
Puzel - 39
Radford - 44,46
Rahn - 21,55,56
Rainge - 53
Ralston - 9
Ramsey - 11,42
Randolph - 31
Rankin - 55
Ray - 56
Rea - 56
Ream - 32
Reaman - 44
Reasman - 44
Reck - 11
Recker - 11
Reed - 1,11,30,42,43,44
Reever - 24
Reid - 8,11,21,50,51
Reif - 16
Reiker - 4
Reinecker - 51
Reinhard - 10,51
Reise - 24
Reiss - 11
Reman - 44

Renshaw - 53,55
Rex - 44
Reynolds - 12,51
Rhea - 52
Rice - 17,39
Richeson - 52
Richie - 10
Rickard - 34
Rickroad - 48
Riddle - 8,9
Riddlemoser - 20,31,53,56
Rider - 20,48
Ried - 9
Rife - 37,45,52
Riff - 10
Riffel - 20
Riffle - 12
Right - 48
Riley - 41
Ripperton - 22
Risk - 52
Ritchey - 21,36
Ritter - 4
Robbinet - 13
Roberts - 48
Robeson - 47
Robinette - 4,12,18,31,35,40,41,55,56
Robinson - 40,50
Robison - 19,31,35,42
Rohrbaugh - 43
Roop - 38
Rope - 52
Rorbaugh - 38
Rose - 20
Ross - 12,31,32,40,42,52,54,55
Rosserman - 50
Rotrought - 32
Roudebush - 41,52
Roudsing - 32
Routson - 21
Routzong - 7
Rowan - 4,22,23,26,32
Rowe - 16
Rudisell - 14,37
Ruffelsbarger - 14
Rummel - 32
Ruommel - 1
Ruperton - 52
Russ - 33
Russell - 1,3,4,5,7,8,9,10,11,12,13,
 14,16,18,20,21,22,23,24,25,
 28,29,30,31,32,36,39,40,42,
 43,44,46,47,49,50,53,54,55,
 56

INDEX

Ryon - 1
Sadler - 10,17
Saeler - 19
Sahn - 16
Sample - 52
Sanble - 17
Sanders - 32,52
Sanderson - 12,21
Saraph - 18
Saum - 12,16
Sawvel - 38
Sax - 52
Sayer - 52
Schane - 32
Schelie - 41
Schlosser - 22,39
Schmeiser - 14
Schmuser - 21
Schnider - 37
Schoener - 18
Schriver - 12,22,32,36,41,42
Scott - 3,4,9,16,24,26,42,56
Scotte - 36
Seabrook - 40
Seabrooke - 40
Seekfriet - 33
Selix - 23
Sell - 27,31,32,45,53,55
Sellers - 1
Semple - 32
Shafter - 49
Shainfelter - 50
Shall - 27,28
Shaller - 37
Shank - 13
Shannon - 53
Shaw - 32
Sheafer - 18
Sheaffer - 17,32
Sheakly - 32
Sheally - 53
Sheckly - 53
Sheely - 41,52,53,55
Sheffer - 17,31,43,44,50,52
Shekely - 28,32
Shekley - 28,49
Shekly - 6,28
Sheldon - 44
Shenfelter - 13
Shenk - 16
Sherer - 36,53
Sherman - 53
Shetron - 53
Shetrone - 45

Shields - 46
Shilt - 22,53
Shimp - 1
Shitz - 7
Sholl - 48
Shopton - 13
Shorb - 12,29,47,48
Shorp - 30
Shorps - 33
Shorrop - 11
Short - 52
Showalter - 45
Shriver - 5,18,20,21,25,32,38,39,
 53,56
Shrock - 32
Shroeder - 43
Shultz - 8,12,15,51
Shusey - 31
Sidsinger - 33
Sief - 33
Sillik - 33
Simund - 33
Sindorf - 5
Sitterown - 53
Skidmore - 7,53
Slagle - 2,4,5,6,8,10,11,21,23,25,31,
 33,34,46,56
Slaybaug - 13
Slaybaugh - 17
Slebaugh - 12
Slee - 40
Slemmens - 19,35
Slemmons - 1,53
Slentz - 43
Slider - 50
Slonecker - 43
Slusser - 14
Slyder - 33,48
Small - 34,55
Smith - 1,3,6,7,9,11,17,18,20,24,26,
 27,28,34,38,42,43,44,47,52,
 53,55,56
Smyser - 35,45
Smyth - 7
Smyzer - 55
Sneer - 53
Sneeringer - 12,22,27,33,39
Snell - 32
Snider - 33,53
Snyder - 4,18,20,23,25,29,43,53,54
Sooter - 12
Soun - 21
Sowers - 22
Spangler - 2,10,47,53

69

INDEX

Speakman - 13,35
Spear - 29,30
Speer - 12,28,56
Spencer - 55
Sponseller - 21
Sprenkle - 54
Spring - 54
Squibb - 13
Stabb - 33
Stallsmith - 47
Stanley - 13
Stapels - 40
Starner - 30
Staub - 25,47
Stauffer - 14
Staulsmith - 20
Staup - 5
Stealy - 54
Steeple - 40
Stehleh - 54
Steigers - 55
Stein - 32,54
Stephens - 10,24,40,41,43,45,49
Sterner - 54
Stevenson - 11,29,36,50
Steveson - 44
Stewart - 8,13,14,20,27,28,29,
33,34,37,42,48,54
Stigers - 34,54
Stine - 25,32
Stivison - 13
Stockslager - 35
Stockslagle - 54
Stockslegar - 13
Stockton - 11
Stoltz - 12,13
Stoner - 13,32,52,54
Storm - 6,25,34,54,55
Stormbaugh - 20
Stotter - 39
Stough - 23
Stout - 1
Stover - 54
Strasbaugh - 30
Strieth - 10
Strome - 18
Strosper - 18
Stuart - 21
Studebaker - 42
Stump - 13
Sturgeon - 6,7,9,25
Summers - 42
Susey - 31
Suttle - 13

Swan - 13
Swartsman - 30
Swartz - 34,41,45
Sweney - 6,9,21,32,34,48,50
Swigart - 34
Swisher - 55
Swope - 1,38,55
Swoyer - 53
Taggart - 28
Tate - 5
Tawney - 25
Tayler - 53
Taylor - 55
Test - 40
Thomas - 12,13,24,33,34,44,52,56
Thompson - 4,7,8,10,12,13,14,22,28,
30,35,39,43,50
Thornburg - 15
Thornburgh - 3,14,55
Timmins - 49
Tomlinson - 35
Toot - 13,55
Topper - 36
Torrence - 13,35,37,41,55
Trimmer - 34
Trine - 13
Trone - 35
Trostle - 45
Troup - 1
Troxell - 16
Trump - 7
Tucker - 35
Turner - 33
Ummer - 46
Underwood - 3,13
Unger - 53
Vanarsdal - 2,19,39
Vanarsdalin - 14
Vandike - 39
Vanest - 19
Vanorsdol - 39
Vanosdallen - 42
Vanscoyce - 35
Vantine - 20
Veely - 2
Waggoner - 4,27,55
Wainbright - 43
Waldebeny - 6
Wales - 6,35
Walker - 3,5,7,13,25,34,35,40,48,50,55
Wallis - 48
Waltemyre - 10
Walter - 11,13,16,34,39,42,43,48,51
Waltman - 35

INDEX

Walsh - 49
Wampler - 43,47
Wardner - 13
Warham - 15
Warner - 33,53
Warnuch - 55
Warren - 30
Wather - 44
Watson - 13,16,47,55
Waugh - 19,21,35,55
Waybright - 18,51,56
Weagle - 54
Weakley - 19,54
Weakly - 35,56
Weaver - 13,14,35,42,56
Webb - 40
Weber - 27
Weems - 56
Weidle - 32
Weidner - 51
Weikart - 18,27
Weikert - 21,24,53
Weirick - 49
Weirman - 5
Weiss - 9
Welk - 46,48,54
Welsh - 8,20,54
Welty - 36
Wentz - 53
Werner - 18,25,26
Werts - 10,14
Wertz - 35,36,48,54
Weyer - 5
Whistler - 25
White - 4,9,10,11,14,18,19,26,
       36,45,49
Whitford - 2
Whitley - 14
Wian - 30
Wible - 36
Wicart - 10
Wickert - 7,39
Wicket - 24
Widner - 51,56
Wieghtner - 14
Wierman - 1,2,3,6,10,14,38,43,51,
         52,55
Wigon - 17
Wikert - 46,56
Wiley - 36
Wilford - 34
Wilkeson - 17,18
Will - 27,29,36,49,54,56
Willet - 14

Williams - 5,7,14,21,24,43,52,56
Williamson - 1,2,36,49
Wills - 39,51
Willson - 3,5,9,49
Wilson - 3,5,8,10,13,14,15,16,24,26,
        28,29,32,34,36,37,38,39,40,
        43,44,48,49,51,52,56,57
Winebright - 1,10,18
Winemiller - 36
Winroth - 36
Winrott - 26,27,33,56
Winterode - 2,16,36,47,48,56
Winteroth - 1
Wintrode - 1,7,26,27,56
Wion - 13
Wireman - 2,15,31,35,36,39,40,44,54
Wirt - 37
Wirtz - 6
Wise - 11,15,55
Wisler - 23
Witherow - 16,19,39,46,50,54
Withrow - 32
Witner - 35
Witt - 41
Wolf - 15,30,31,33,36,41,47,56
Wolford - 56
Wollet - 1
Wollett - 8
Wolverton - 50
Woolf - 38
Work - 36
Workman - 13,40
Worley - 14,21
Worst - 37
Wortz - 51
Woutz - 38
Wray - 34,51,52
Wright - 3,4,5,14,20,24,33,34,36,44,
        49,52,57
Wunder - 54
Wyble - 26
Yeagy - 40,43,44,45
Yetts - 36,52
Young - 15,20,23,37,55
Zacharias - 13
Zeigler - 18
Zell - 37
Zettle - 57
Zeyer - 13,19
Ziegler - 5,20,36,45
Zimmerman - 11,46,48,51
Zolinger - 51
Zoosserman - 5

INDEX

Additional entries:

Beeher - 25   Nickly - 50

www.ingramcontent.com/pod-product-compliance
Lightning Source LLC
LaVergne TN
LVHW051708080426
835511LV00017B/2800